To Ext

Patagonian Odyssey

A Travel Memoir

by
Bill MacDonald

Bill McDonald

Dec /02

"The borderline between fiction and non-fiction is extremely arbitrary, and invented by publishers."

—Bruce Chatwin

"To pass off fiction as reality, or to inject fiction into reality, is one of the most demanding and imperishable of human enterprises – and the dearest ambition of any storyteller."

—Mario Vargas Llosa

For Catherine, obviously.

Patagonian Odyssey

A Travel Memoir

by

Bill MacDonald

BOREALIS
BOOK PUBLISHERS

Borealis Press Ltd.
Ottawa, Canada
2001

Canadä

*The Publishers acknowledge the financial assistance
of the Government of Canada through the Book Publishing
Industry Development Program (BPIDP)
for our publishing activities*

National Library of Canada Cataloguing in Publication Data

MacDonald, Bill, 1932-
    Patagonian Odyssey

ISBN 0-88887-184-8

    1. MacDonald, Bill, 1932—Journeys—Patagonia
(Argentina and Chile) 2. Patagonia (Argentina and Chile)—
Description and travel. I. Title.

F2817.M33 2001   918.2'70464   C2001-902645-5

Cover design by Bull's Eye Design, Ottawa
Typesetting by Chisholm Communications, Ottawa
Photos by Bill MacDonald

Printed and bound in Canada on acid-free paper

Coquimbo

San Juan

Cerro Aconcagua
Mendoza

Valparaíso

SANTIAGO

San Rafael

Chillán

Concepción

Valdivia

Bariloche

Puerto Montt

Chiloé

*ARCHIPÉLAGO DE
LOS CHONOS*

**PACIFIC
OCEAN**

Wellington

*ARCHIPÉLAGO
REINA ADELAIDE*

Santa Inés

Punta Arenas

SIERRA DE CÓRDOB

Córdoba

Concordia

Rosario

URUGUAY

PAMPAS

**BUENOS
AIRES**

A R G E N T I N A

Salado

Mar del Plata

Bahía Blanca

Colorado

Negro

Limay

Viedma

Peninsula Valdés

Chubut

Rawson

Comodoro Rivadavia

Deseado

Puerto Deseado

Chico

Puerto Santa Cruz

Río Gallegos

Strait of Magellan

Tierra del Fuego

Cape Horn

C H I L E

**ATLANTIC
OCEAN**

*Falkland Islands
Islas Malvinas*

N

| 0 | 500 km |
| 0 | 300 miles |

Table of Contents

Chapter 1.

At Ushuaia Prison

"Ushuaia began with a prefabricated mission house put up in 1869 alongside the shacks of Yaghan Indians. Then the Argentine Navy came and the Indians died of measles and pneumonia. The settlement graduated from navy base to convict station. The Inspector of Prisons designed a masterpiece. It is now used as a barracks."
—Bruce Chatwin: *In Patagonia*

On a gray September afternoon, aboard a jam-packed Aerolíneas Argentinas jet, I flew south from Buenos Aires to Bahía Blanca, halfway down Argentina's Atlantic coast. From Bahía Blanca, I continued due south to the seaside town of Río Gallegos, where all but a dozen passengers disembarked. Watching them leave, I had the feeling they were looking at me sympathetically, as though implying that venturing any closer to Cape Horn would be foolhardy. Daylight was fading, clouds had dropped below the mountaintops, fog was rolling in from the direction of the Falkland Islands. Not only that, civilization pretty well ended at Río Gallegos, unless you counted Fuegian fishermen and a few untamed guanacos.

Nevertheless, I still had three hundred kilometres to go, and the two cocky young pilots, hardly more than teenagers, despite their smart caps and mustaches, seemed determined to press on. Which is what we did. An hour and a half later, after descending into a maze of steep-sided, mist-shrouded valleys, and (it seemed to me) searching desperately for a place to land, we touched down at the remote Patagonian outpost of Ushuaia, on the bleak, inhospitable island of Tierra del Fuego. Disembarking at dusk under snowcapped mountains, buffeted by a sleety gale howling in off the Beagle Channel, I was reminded of winter nights in northern British Columbia.

Both the cab driver and the desk clerk at the Hotel Albatross asked me if I were on my way to Antarctica. When I said no, I wasn't, they assumed I was a marine biologist, come to study elephant seals or penguins. When I denied any interest in biology or polar exploration, they were stymied. "Then why you coming all these way to Ushuaia, señor?"

To the cab driver I said simply, "I wanted to see if Bruce Chatwin was telling the truth about Patagonia."

To Leandro, the bilingual desk clerk, who offered me a room on the top floor of the Albatross, overlooking Ushuaia harbour, I said, "It's a long story. I've come to see my grandfather's final resting place. He died here in 1924."

Perhaps I should explain:

In the fall of 1914, Grampa MacDonald, a swash-buckling marine wireless operator, prone to brawling in barrooms, sailed out of Halifax aboard the package freighter *Duchess of Albany.* They were bound for the Argentine port of Mar del Plata and their cargo consisted mainly of mining machinery and farm tractors. From Mar del Plata they were to proceed to Punta Alta, fill their holds with tanned horse hides and raw wool, then return to Halifax.

Unfortunately for Grampa MacDonald, and for Grandma as well, at home with two small children, fate had other plans. On a starry night in Mar del Plata, with the Southern Cross reflected in the harbour, the officers of the *Duchess of Albany* repaired to a portside hotel called the Cabo Blanco, to share a noggin and steady their sea legs. They drank whisky and gin, listened to gaucho guitars, danced with sultry ladies of the evening. Since the moored ship had no need of her radio, Grampa MacDonald, well into his cups, elected to spend the night in the stationary comfort of the Cabo Blanco.

Toward morning, in the fetid, curtainless room where he was sleeping, he was rudely awakened by a belligerent group of unshaven policemen brandishing truncheons.

"Get up, murderer!" they shouted at him, whacking him about the head and shoulders, pulling him roughly out of bed.

At first, he was not unduly concerned. He had, after all, been manhandled by the law a time or two during his career. But when he discovered that he was alone, that none of his shipmates were in the hotel, or even ashore, and when he was dragged bodily into the adjoining room and saw a bloated, bald-headed man on the floor with his skull crushed, he began to be afraid. Especially when the sneering policemen pointed accusing fingers at the apparent bloodstains on Grampa's hands.

"These are battery acid stains, you stupid bastards!" he must have shouted. "Dilute sulphuric battery acid stains. All marine radio operators have them."

But of course the policemen didn't know what he was saying. Nor, had they known, would they have believed him. After being allowed to put on his socks and underwear, he was handcuffed and conveyed to a nearby jailhouse, where he was thrown into a squalid cell. Unable to speak Spanish, he could neither protest his innocence nor determine exactly what it was his captors deemed him guilty of.

He was visited that evening by two people. The first, he deduced, was some sort of magistrate, who told him in barely comprehensible English that he was accused of callously bashing in the brains of a prominent city functionary, señor Rivadavia, for no other reason than robbery, or perhaps jealousy, and that the courts could easily prove that señor Rivadavia was not in the habit of frequenting prostitutes at waterfront bordellos. Grampa MacDonald failed to grasp the logic of these incriminations.

The other person to visit him in jail that night was first mate Rossetti, from the *Duchess of Albany,* sent by the captain to inform him that they would weigh anchor at daybreak and depart for Punta Alta on the morning tide. If he were not cleared of charges by then, they would be obliged to strike his name from the roster and sail without him. Rossetti said, "It appears, my friend, that señor Rivadavia was a respected civic official, and what's required now, to quash a scandal and prevent an investigation, is a quick, plausible solution. You, I'm afraid, are the designated scapegoat."

It was at this point, I believe, that Grampa MacDonald began to take the situation very seriously. Especially when the magistrate reappeared and informed him that a reliable prostitute had identified him as the assailant she'd seen hammering señor Rivadavia on the head with a crockery pitcher. How else, demanded the magistrate, could he explain those obvious bloodstains on his fingers?

Grampa shouted and bellowed at the magistrate in English, shook him by the shoulders, threatened to claw the accusatory smirk off his face. But the magistrate only laughed and called him a lunatic. Then two gaolers in greasy uniforms came and rescued the magistrate and ordered Grampa to be quiet, under threat of severe physical restraint.

Grampa must have thought sadly about his home in Cumberland County then, about his wife and babies, and wondered how long it would be until he saw them. He must have regretted ever having sailed from Halifax aboard the *Duchess of Albany,* ever having stepped ashore in Mar del Plata, on Argentina's northeast coast. Exhausted by anger and frustration, alone, afraid, he did something he hadn't done since childhood: he put his face in his hands and wept.

In February, 1915, Grampa MacDonald and fifty other felons were shackled and placed aboard the prison ship *Primero de Mayo.* On a hot, windy morning they set sail from Mar del Plata, bound for the isolated penal colony at Ushuaia, nine hundred miles due south, on the mountainous island of Tierra del Fuego. The voyage took five days against fierce headwinds, during which time my grandfather was seasick for the first time in his life. As were all the other convicts. A coop of live chickens was washed overboard. Two hysterical Chileans, tethered below decks in the coal bunker, died of fright and dehydration.

If Grampa wrote letters home during his incarceration at Mar del Plata, which seems likely, they did not arrive. The first my grandmother knew of his predicament was when the master of the *Duchess of Albany,* a Newfoundlander named Cowlthorp, sent her a parcel of Grampa's personal effects from St. John's, with a note saying he hoped things would soon be sorted out.

Not knowing what else to do, Grandma MacDonald went to the Cumberland County Police Commissioner, who referred her to the Argentine Consulate in Ottawa, who put her in touch with the Canadian Consulate in Buenos Aires, who took four months to inform her that her husband, duly tried and convicted of manslaughter in a Court of Law, had been summarily sentenced to ten years at hard labour. A spousal visit, they assured her, given global circumstances, was unthinkable. Nor could they provide details of her husband's arraignment, except to say that as far as they knew, he had been defended by a qualified, if inexperienced lawyer. Unfortunately, as she herself must realize, with international hostilities raging in Europe, their diplomatic duties left them little time for private, civilian investigations.

In June of 1916, after she had almost given up hope, Grandma MacDonald received her first letter from Ushuaia Prison. In it, Grampa told her of the storm-wracked voyage from Mar del Plata, of the cruel desolation of Tierra del Fuego, of life behind bars in the cold, dark cell block. He told her of back-breaking labour cracking stones and digging drainage ditches, of beatings endured for not understanding what the guards were saying.

He longed, he said, for word from her. Would she please write and let him know if any of his previous letters had reached her. Would she please send books, and photographs of the children. If there was any hope of survival, he said, it lay in learning enough Spanish to appease the guards and communicate with his fellow inmates. In exchange, he said, he had offered to teach English to anyone interested, but so far not a soul had come forward. He said he hoped soon to be included in a work party building a narrow-gauge railway west of the encampment, because he needed fresh air and sunshine. Prison swill, he said, made from maggoty potatoes and rancid bully beef, was inadequate, even when supplemented by fish obtained from the locals. He longed for mincemeat tarts and a decent cup of tea. "How, my love, will I last ten years in this place, ten years without seeing you or the children? How will I stay alive as daylight fades and snow buries this miserable bastille? How will I preserve the spark of life, how retain my sanity? There is no one here to whom I can proclaim my innocence. My queries are ignored, my complaints scoffed at. My very presence seems resented. And if I understand the carcelero correctly, ten years is but a minimum sentence. That is not what I was told by the tribunal in Mar del Plata. I could be here forever."

Between 1916 and 1924, Grandma MacDonald received a total of three letters from Ushuaia. They were written in pencil on coarse brown paper, haphazardly censored, difficult to decipher. Whether Grampa MacDonald wrote more than three letters is difficult to say.

Not that these sad, infrequent communications, full of fear and foreboding, did anything to ease Grandma's pain. For days after their arrival she would confine herself to bed and suffer silent anguish. It took weeks for her sorrow to give way to anger, her anger to resignation. Pleadings to the Argentine Consulate went unanswered. As early as 1918 she began to be tormented by a recurring dream, in which she saw Grampa MacDonald standing at the front door with a headless corpse in his arms. On one occasion her brother, dour Uncle Edgar, on medical leave from the army, had her sedated and committed to the Gull's Wing Sanatorium for emotional therapy.

And then in December of 1924, on the same day the *Duchess of Albany*, still under the command of Captain Cowlthorp, sank in a fierce winter storm off the coast of Cape Breton, Grandma MacDonald received a typewritten letter, on Presidio de Ushuaia stationery, from a certain carcelero Ezeiza, expressing official regret that she was now a widow. "I must sadly say you, señora, that your marido, señor MacDonald, lose his life by pulmonia of the lungs. Our estimar doctor médico pronounce this, nothing can save pulmonia. Is enterred your marido, I must sadly say you, in cementerio de Ushuaia, which is nice tumba with grasses. Is regret also estimar capellán Carlos, oblige as myself."

Grandma forwarded copies of Ezeiza's message to the Argentine Consulate in Ottawa, requesting clarification, and to the Canadian Consulate in Buenos Aires, demanding at least a death certificate. Both times, perhaps because diplomatic relations were strained and people preoccupied, her pleadings were ignored. Eventually she pasted Ezeiza's document inside her wedding album, along with Grampa's heartbreaking letters from Ushuaia prison. There, to this day, it remains.

Apparently Uncle Edgar was the only one who ranted and raved much. Which was odd, because all his life he'd disliked Grampa MacDonald, had thought him a footloose cad. He advanced the idiotic theory that sly Grampa had never spent a day behind bars at Ushuaia, that he was alive and well on some vast estancia in the pampas, probably with a rich mistress, riding around on a black stallion all day, spending his nights drinking and dancing. No one took this seriously, least of all Grandma MacDonald, because they all knew it was the sort of romantic existence Uncle Edgar himself craved, but lacked the courage to seek. And of course there were Grampa's letters from Ushuaia prison, for which Uncle Edgar could offer no explanation.

Speaking of letters, the last one Grandma ever received from Patagonia arrived on Christmas Eve, 1928. It had been written in fractured English by an ex-convict named Horacio

Mendoza, who now tended sheep and led a quiet life at Calafate, near the Perito Moreno glacier. The reason he was writing, he said, was that during the postwar years he had occupied the cell next to señor MacDonald's, and in that time they had become friends. Señor MacDonald, he said, was a kind man, a courageous man, who, after he learned to speak Spanish, amused his fellow inmates with stories of Canada and the high seas. In the evenings, after labouring all day on the narrow-gauge railway, señor MacDonald would conduct English lessons. Which was how he himself had begun to learn the language, as had several others, including a number of guards. Inmates tended to respect señor MacDonald because he had killed a man with his bare hands in Mar del Plata. Some insect of a port official named Rivadavia. Mendoza's own crime, that of stealing and selling his employer's cattle, paled in comparison with the courageous, bare-fisted exploit of señor MacDonald.

Horacio Mendoza said he wondered what warden Ezeiza had told Grandma, if anything, concerning her husband's death. The truth was, he had cut himself severely on the leg with an axe one day, right down to the bone, while chopping trees along the railroad. By week's end putrefaction had set in. There were rumours that someone else had cut him, deliberately. An enemy, perhaps, though Horacio doubted this, because señor MacDonald had no enemies. In any event, raging fever had followed, accompanied by a horrible smell and bronchial convulsions, worse than tuberculosis, which rendered the patient so delirious he mistook the stripes on his tunic for poisonous snakes. Eleven days later, in a pathetic, unconscious state, due to lack of medical attention, the poor man had expired.

"I must say you, señora," wrote Mendoza, "your husband is my good amigo friend. One day on the railroad track he find these rabbit with teethmarks of a fox, and he keep these rabbit in his cell for one moth, and it not die. But is terrible axeman, now is bury under ground, someone eat these rabbit. Ushuaia prison close maybe someday, dispose by El Presidente. In Calafate I am shearing these sheep, drinking maté, but your husband is my always good amigo friend."

One nice thing about the Hotel Albatross, on Ushuaia's windy waterfront, is that on its ground floor resides the very helpful Instituto Fuegino de Turismo. After a good night's sleep, lulled by foghorns, I stopped in at the Institute and asked for information on northern Patagonia. Frederico, the chubby little man in shirt-sleeves behind the counter, recommended a visit to the lakeside town of Bariloche, which he said would remind me of Aspen, Colorado. I said I'd never been to Aspen, Colorado. Frederico looked shocked. An American who hadn't been to Aspen, Colorado? Imagine that. Well, one must also keep in mind that Bariloche was where many famous Nazis had taken refuge. And if that didn't interest me, there was always the scenery: the lakes, the mountains, the ski resorts. Yes, but was it possible to enter Chile from there? Quite possible, he thought. He didn't know exactly how, but was reasonably sure it could be done. Should he reserve me a seat on Kaikén Air for the day after tomorrow? Good idea. But why Kaikén Air? Why not Aerolíneas Argentinas? Well, because, for one thing, Aerolíneas Argentinas had no planes flying from Ushuaia to Bariloche. That might pose a problem, mightn't it? Fortunately for me, though, and for Frederico, who got a commission, Kaikén Air did have planes. Not every day. Possibly every second day or third day. He would have to check. At least it was better than no planes at all.

Another nice thing about the Hotel Albatross is that from it, if you know where to look, you can see the shattered red bricks and black tin roof of the old prison's one remaining cell block. It clings to the rocky hillside just east of town, enclosed by wire fences and a crumbling stone wall. The other two cell blocks, as well as the laundry, latrine and blacksmith shop, were torn down by the Argentine Navy in 1949 to make room for a parade square. Various other buildings were also demolished, and the dilapidated prison cemetery was paved over to make a military parking lot.

Walking uphill in wind and morning drizzle, I was aware of being stared at by townspeople in the narrow, unpaved streets. Not that they were unfriendly, only curious. At the gates of the naval compound I was stopped by a short, almost dwarfish sailor, who asked the purpose of my visit.

"I've come to see the prison."

"Eez no prison."

"The old cell block."

"Eez close, these old cell block."

"I understood it was open to the public, as a tourist attraction."

Thrusting out his chin, the sailor gave me a suspicious, challenging look. "Err you these tourist?"

"Of course I'm a tourist. What else would I be?"

"Show me these passport."

After scrutinizing my passport and shrugging his thin shoulders, he demanded an admission fee of three pesos. Plus my camera, for safekeeping. "No picture allow these prison." A cold, gusty rain was falling, forming puddles at our feet, and so I gave him three pesos and my camera and splashed across the parade square toward the cell block.

It was a dark, forbidding, cavernous mausoleum, much larger than it had appeared from a distance. There were two galleries of twenty cells each, one above the other, with rusty iron doors hanging open, as though the inmates were away on day pass. Halfway down the corridor, on whose uneven floor lay decades of bird droppings, stood a decomposed tin stove with rusty pipes rising through the roof, evidently the only source of heat. I wondered if Grampa MacDonald's cell had been anywhere near it. Or, for that matter, if this had really been his cell block.

I remember the smells of rot, mildew, damp mortar. It occurred to me that the bricks on the exterior were only a veneer—the building was made of stone and concrete. In the lower gallery, some cells had floors of packed earth, others of filthy lumber. Their narrow windows were so opaque with dirt that little light penetrated. I stood in the dank, oppressive gloom, listening for convicts' voices. I saw no table at which my grandfather might have written his pathetic letters, no bench on which he and his friend Mendoza might have sat and talked. While I stood there, shivering, the dwarfish sailor from the gatehouse came wandering through. When he saw me he stopped and lit himself a cigarette.

"Whose idea was it to preserve this particular cell block?" I asked him.

But he didn't answer, only stood there smoking and staring at me. I wondered if he even realized that this had once been a prison, that for half a century it had housed Argentina's worst criminals. Or perhaps that was his problem: he could not quite bring himself to forgive the awful transgressions committed by those who had once lived and died here.

"Will they ever make this into a proper museum?" I asked. "Display old tools, old artifacts? Put up a list of names?"

Still silent, glaring at me with what I took to be hostility, the sailor threw down the remains of his cigarette, ground it under his heel.

"Are you by any chance descended from a long line of turnkeys?" I asked him as he walked back toward his post at the gatehouse. "Or are you afraid I'll steal the leg irons?"

It was then I perceived that I was not alone. At the end of the upper gallery, stepping out of the shadows, appeared a young woman in a dark skirt and faded orange jacket. She wore a white knitted hat and a dark scarf. She was carrying a handbag and a sheathed umbrella. The moment I saw her I understood why the sailor, feeling thwarted by my presence, had seemed less than attentive. She descended the iron staircase slowly, cautiously, and approached me. So as to let her know I didn't speak Spanish, I greeted her in English, made an idiotic comment about the atrocious weather, asked her what she was doing. "Mi abuelo," she said, "my maternal grandpapa, spend fifteen years in these cell. Eez where he die.

From Bariloche, my mother bring me here, before I understand. Now I come back. The guard has warn me no go upstair. Eez rope off. But I go anyway. You are these American tourist."

It wasn't a question, so I said nothing. I thought she might be a secretary, or a flight attendant. She gazed up at the cells above us, shook her head, started to cry. She was a year or two younger than I'd first thought, dark-haired, quite attractive, taller than the sailor. Her cheeks were red from the cold and her nose was running. "This is bad place," she said, sniffling. "Ugly place. So dark. I think my grandfather watch me."

"I was just leaving," I said.

"You are lucky person no hab these sad memory. You are foreign tourist. You don' know these thing."

"Maybe so, but still, it's been worth the price of admission."

She looked surprised. "You pay these money to come in?"

"I did. I paid the guard three pesos."

"Eez no necessary! Eez free. Eez no entry." She shook her head, rolled her eyes. "I say him my grandpapa dies here."

We crossed the vacant parade square in the rain, our faces so wet you couldn't tell who was crying and who wasn't. In the relentless wind off the ocean, raising an umbrella would have been futile. The dwarfish sailor, sulking in his rainproof gatehouse, coping with unfulfilled fantasies, lit a cigarette and gave me back my camera. When I offered to take his picture, he strode menacingly toward me, waving his cap in my face. "Eez no allow! Eez no permiso!"

As the girl and I backed off and hurried away, she offered me her hand in farewell, mistakenly assuming I was anxious to leave and had somewhere to go, when actually I wanted to stay with her. The thought of returning alone to the Hotel Albatross was depressing.

"My name is Maria Malaspina," she said brightly, hugging herself, brushing raindrops off her hair. "Muchas gracias for no laugh at me. I like to buy you drinks on these rainy day, if you are in no such a hurry. I stay at the Albatross Hotel, which hab these ber' nice lounge and ber' nice fire-place and these hot grog rum if you visit me. Eez no far. Is ber' nice on these rainy day."

"Indeed," I said. "By all means. I couldn't agree more. I was about to suggest it myself, if you hadn't."

She laughed as I took her arm and her umbrella. I was surprised at how warm her hand was when she allowed me to hold it. Turning our backs for good on the dwarfish, scowling sailor, whose problems included nicotine addiction and tak-ing himself too seriously, we began our descent, down through the same narrow, misty streets I had negotiated ear-lier. This time, though, I didn't mind being stared at by the passersby, who, despite wind and rain and the proximity of Ushuaia prison, were happy enough with life to be smiling.

Striding along, holding my hand, Maria Malaspina said, "So, you know these Hotel Albatross?"

"Oh, I do indeed. Strange as it may seem, I'm very famil-iar with the Hotel Albatross."

Heavy clouds moved in as the afternoon wore on, obscuring nearby mountain peaks and bringing squalls of rain. At dusk, sleet rattled against the hotel windows, driven by howling gusts. The Beagle Channel seethed with whitecaps and we watched a snub-nosed supply ship heave its ponderous way shoreward.

In the lounge of the Hotel Albatross, with a fire crackling in the fireplace and an affable bartender willing to mix hot grogs, Maria and I were the only patrons. Earlier there had been a noisy group of Bolivian backpackers, angry at the storm, but as soon as they ran out of money for drinks, they departed. As darkness fell, we watched a distant lighthouse begin flashing at the entrance to Ushuaia Harbour. At the edge of the known world, according to Maria, beyond which lay nothing but black, empty space.

She worked for a prominent realtor in Bariloche, where she'd lived all her life, except for a year in Buenos Aires and two semesters as an exchange student in Panama. Her faith-less husband, Luis, whose wedding band she wore, but from whom she was temporarily separated, was copilot on an Aus-tral Airlines cargo plane. As a matter of fact, on the weekend, Luis was flying across the Andes from Puerto Natales in Chile to join her and attempt yet another reconciliation. Did she hold out much hope? Some, but not much. Luis had girl-friends in every airport, on both sides of the Andes. Maybe if they had a child together, things would improve. On the weekend, she might, or might not try to conceive one. It all depended. Who could predict? Life in Argentina these days was strange and unpredictable.

"Not just in Argentina," I said, and told her I knew from bitter experience exactly how it felt when a marriage disinte-grated.

But what she really wanted to talk about was neither mar-riage nor the privatization politics of President Carlos Menem. She was not even interested in the musical, *Evita*. All of these were fine in their place, but she was most anxious to tell me about her maternal grandfather, Rico Benzacar, the man who had died in Ushuaia prison. It seems that señor Benzacar, her mother's beloved father, had been a devout and active participant in Antonio Soto's anarchist rebellion of 1921. To prove his devotion, he had ruthlessly trussed up an estancia owner in ropes, taken him to the top of Bariloche's highest mountain, and, after performing certain mutilations, had thrown the scoundrel to his death on the rocks below. In front of witnesses. At his trial, after dismissing his attorney as a capitalist nincompoop, he not only bragged of his evil deed, but said he'd do it again, under comparable circumstances, as a matter of principle.

Though it pained Maria to tell it, and necessitated a num-ber of hot grogs, I enjoyed her story. She smiled when I praised her self-sufficient grandfather, Rico Benzacar, and commiser-ated with her over his lengthy and fatal imprisonment.

She peered through her empty glass at the fire, and out the window at the distant lighthouse, flashing its warning at the edge of the universe. "The man he throw off these Cathedral Mountain, señor Roque, eez presidente of these sociedad patriotico. So you see, eez no such a good idea to do these."

I caught the bartender's eye and signalled for fresh grogs. Wind and rain buffeted the windows in front of us, but what did it matter? I thought of the dark, decaying cells I'd seen that morning, the sad cells of Ushuaia prison. I pitied poor Grampa MacDonald and his loyal friend, Horacio Mendoza. I pitied Grandma, who had waited in vain. I pitied Captain Cowlthorp, drowned at sea with all his men. I even pitied Rico Benzacar, the anarchist.

I rather expected we'd talk about that half-tamed Fuegian, Jemmy Button. Or about his abductor, Captain FitzRoy, of H.M.S. *Beagle*. Or about his biographer, Charles Darwin. I thought Maria might have mentioned that famous French aviator, Antoine de Saint-Exupéry, her husband's hero, who had opened up the airmail routes in Patagonia about the time her dissident grandfather was tossing people off Cathedral Mountain.

"You hab no idea," she whispered, holding my hand for comfort, "what eez like to see the cell of your grandpapa, where he spend eez life and dies these horrible death."

She was crying again. It had certainly been a day for crying. The solicitous bartender put aromatic logs of pine and cedar on the fire, brought us a tray of drinks. Still holding my hand, Maria said, "Now eez your turn. Now you muz tell me why you come to Patagonia. No for los pingüinos?"

"No," I said. "Not for the pingüinos. I'm afraid I'm like the Ancient Mariner, condemned to a life of aimless wandering."

She looked at me suspiciously. "You are these drug pusher?"

"No, I'm no drug pusher."

"You are marry? You hab these wife?"

"No. Not anymore."

"You are on these holiday?"

"Not exactly."

"What, then? You telling me, por favor."

The bartender, without being asked, laid a starched white cloth on our table. He lit candles, set out silverware for supper, handed us menus and a wine list. I watched candlelight dance in Maria's eyes. "Shall I tell you the real reason? You'll never believe me."

"Sí, sí, sí!," she said, glancing at the window as a particularly heavy shower of rain hit it, accompanied by a tremendous gust of wind. "You tell me, I believe it."

I could think of nowhere else I'd rather be at that moment. The waiter uncorked a bottle of Cousiño-Macul, filled our glasses, exhorted, "Buen provecho!"

I touched my glass to Maria's. "Salud!" I said, and proceeded to tell her exactly why I'd come to Ushuaia.

* * *

Chapter 2.

Across the Andes by Bus & Boat, from Bariloche, on the shores of Lago Nahuel Huapi, to Puerto Montt, on the Gulf of Ancud.

If there'd been a train running from Ushuaia to northern Patagonia, I might have taken it, just to view the scenery. But since there wasn't, I flew. Beset by the strange feeling that I'd forgotten something, that I'd be back someday, I boarded a Kaikén Airlines turboprop and endured a four hour nonstop flight to Bariloche, on the shores of Lake Nahuel Huapi. The flight would have taken longer, supposedly, but for the favourable tailwinds helping us along.

Despite Frederico's plug, Bariloche, a resort town of ninety thousand in the centre of Parque Nacional Nahuel Huapi and gateway to the Argentine lake district, was not my destination of choice. What I planned was nothing more than a brief stopover while I figured out how to traverse the Andes into Chile without having to go all the way north to Santiago.

I took a room at the Hotel Eidelweiss, enjoyed a good dinner and a good sleep, and the following day, after an hour's sleuthing at the Centro Cívico, found out from exuberant señora Aluminé how this could be done. (It was señora Aluminé's last day on the job. She'd been promoted, or demoted, to the head office in Buenos Aires, and that's why she had lots of time for me.)

First, she would sell me a bus ticket to Puerto Pañuelo, where I would board the ferryboat that sailed every second day down Lago Nahuel Huapi to Puerto Frías. At Puerto Frías, I would board a 4WD bus for a short trip through craggy precipices to the remote Chilean border post at Paso de Pérez Rosales. From there, assuming they let me in, I would board a second 4WD bus which would grind and slither its way through steep gorges to the mountain village of Peulla. Here, thanks to a personal phone call from señora Aluminé (no extra charge, except for the call itself), I would be welcomed for the night at the rustic Hostería Peulla. In the morning, or sometime before noon, weather and fog permitting, I would board yet another ferryboat and navigate Lago Todos los Santos to the Chilean hill town of Petrohué. Señora Aluminé wasn't sure (indeed, had no idea) what time of day I'd arrive at Petrohué, but hopefully before nightfall. If such was the case, I would then proceed by express bus downhill past the silent but nervous Volcán Calbuco. Thence, God willing, to Puerto Varas, and finally, O joy! to Puerto Montt, my intended destination. Ebullient señora Aluminé conceded that this trip might seem a tad complicated, but assured me that bouncing uphill and down through the rain forest, under tall, heavy-crowned coihue trees, surrounded at all times by spectacular Andean scenery, would more than offset any inconvenience. Did she know of anyone who had actually effectuated this exact itinerary? Well, yes. Many people. Not so many in September as in January and February, when travellers took their summer holidays, but still, the trip was not uncommon. After consulting her maps and brochures, she saw no reason why an adventurous person such as myself should not enjoy it. Oh, and if I did accomplish it, perhaps I might send her a postcard, in care of the Secretaría Municipal de Turismo in Buenos Aires, with recommendations, so that she could further publicize this transalpine route to other tourists. It would be helpful if I mentioned the cost, which was something people liked to know, especially backpackers.

The highest cat I've ever seen, in terms of elevation above sea level, was at that Chilean Customs post at Paso de Pérez Rosales in the Andes, 900 kilometres south of Santiago. There, on a precipitous, desolate hillside, in the midst of axle-deep mud puddles, we were ordered to disembark with our pass-

By bus over the Andes from Argentina to Chile.

ports and undergo interrogation.

The Customs building was cold, damp, poorly lit. Our nostrils were assailed by the smells of stale tobacco and faulty plumbing. And yet, as with most border guards, these self-conscious, unsmiling men, wearing ragtag uniforms and badly in need of cologne, were obviously puffed up with their own importance. They scrutinized our credentials, went through our luggage, looking for God knows what. They may simply have been curious to see what we had. Envy may have played a part. It seemed to me they took longer examining the women's suitcases than the men's, running their dirty hands through the underwear, holding items up to the dim, watery light. Momentarily, I had the sensation of being admitted to a mental institution, rather than to a country supposedly eager for tourists.

In the midst of all this, as we stood in line waiting to be processed, a large, ivory-coloured cat came wandering through. Its fur was the shade of old piano keys. It had large feet, pale green eyes and slightly tufted ears, as though one of its ancestors might have been a cougar. The trouble I have with cats, no matter where I meet them, is that I want them to like me. Which is why I always extend a hand and try to make contact. If they let me, I'll pet them, scratch them behind the ears. If they prefer a less demonstrative relationship, I can live with that, so long as we exchange pleasantries. Some cats are by nature aloof and do not entirely trust strangers. It may be something in their genes, left over from a time when members of the Felidae race were persecuted.

This ivory Chilean cat, however, responded to my advances like a long lost lover. When I clucked my tongue and said, "Puss, Puss, Puss," it ran right to me. Without a moment's hesitation it leapt up onto the long wooden table upon which our luggage lay, and rewarded me by rubbing its cheek passionately against my outstretched hand. Not content with that, it then stood up, put its forepaws against my chest, and before I had time to guess its intentions, climbed into my arms. Which of course I didn't mind. Since I wasn't going anywhere, I stood there like a father cradling an infant, and was aware of people smiling. It occurred to me that the Customs officers would have done well to take lessons in hospitality from their mascot, who was vigorously buffing the underside of my chin with the top of its head and purring like a gravel crusher. I had never heard a cat purr so loudly. Its whole body vibrated. People at both ends of the inspection line turned to see where the noise was coming from.

When it was finally my turn to be examined, I was still holding the cat. Jokingly, I said, "Is this your special drug-sniffing cat?" But the surly agent thumbing through my passport neither smiled nor said anything. It may be that he didn't understand English. Never once did we make eye contact. Watching him go through my clothes and toiletries, I felt mildly violated. When he came to my supply of insulin and needles, he held them up gingerly, as though they were explosives. Still not looking at me, he rattled off a barrage of questions in Spanish.

"Diabetes," I said, and showed him my Medic Alert bracelet.

Not satisfied, he spoke sharply to one of his colleagues, who came over and had a look too. They seemed undecided, until suddenly the first officer scooped up all my paraphernalia, set it aside, and shook his head at me. Then he wagged his finger disapprovingly. I was half expecting him to draw his revolver. Instead, he fired off a salvo in Spanish, which sounded more like threats than questions. During all this, he never once looked directly at me. I was aware of an ominous silence, interspersed with the cat's loud purrs and the grumblings of my fellow travellers, who were growing impatient at the delay.

Finally a hawkish, grey-haired woman behind me, wearing hiking boots and festooned with cameras and binoculars, said something to the guard in Spanish. I detected the word "diabetic" several times. At long last, and very reluctantly, the guard stuffed my needles and bottles of insulin into my backpack, pushed it disdainfully toward me, shoved my passport into my hand. Visibly irritated, spitting his cigarette out on the floor, he motioned at me to move on. I suppose had he wanted to, he could have turned me away, sent me back to Argentina. Or demanded a fee. I wanted to ask him whether he objected to tourists in general entering his country, or just insulin dependent ones.

Not until we were back outside in the mist did I realize I was still holding the ivory cat. Now, though it was still purring, it seemed to be asleep. So I disengaged its claws from my sweater and placed it on a bench outside the Customs office, among a group of dirty-faced urchins who were chattering at us in Spanish and holding out their palms.

I obtained Chilean pesos through the barred windows of a small casa de cambio attached to the Customs post. As I prepared to board the bus that would take me down to Peulla and the rustic hostería, I became aware that people were laughing at me. How cruel, I thought, to mock another's misfortune. Then the thin woman with the cameras and binoculars said, "Look your sweater, señor."

When I glanced down I saw that the front of my wooly black sweater, which I'd worn in case the trip over the Andes proved chilly, was solidly covered with ivory-coloured cat hair. I looked as though I'd just climbed out of a snowbank, or spilled a carton of milk down my chest.

It took days to pluck off all those hairs, which clung like chinchilla. Not that I worked very hard at removing them. As I travelled the rest of the way down to Puerto Montt and the Pacific Ocean, they reminded me of the friendly cat who had welcomed me so warmly at the border.

* * *

Chapter 3.

From Puerto Montt to Puerto Aguirre, en route to Laguna San Rafael.

It had been my intention all along to spend a few days in the Chilean coastal town of Puerto Montt, on the Golfo de Ancud, a thousand kilometres south of Santiago. In population, Puerto Montt (founded in 1852 and named after President Manuel Montt) is about the same size as Lake Superior's Thunder Bay, Ontario. It bears other similarities too, relying as it does on logging, shipping and rail traffic. Like Thunder Bay, it's built along the waterfront and has its quota of off-shore islands, docks and warehouses. Wooded hills rise behind it, giving it the shape and appearance of Duluth, Minnesota. Though fairly prosperous, it's a blue collar town, a working port, and makes up in vitality what it lacks in glamour. Like Duluth and Thunder Bay, Puerto Montt is neither squeaky clean nor prettily manicured. It smells and sounds like a salt water harbour, not a sissified marina. Everywhere you go you hear engines: trains, ships, trucks. When the wind is onshore, you detect the tang of the sea. Though Duluth and Thunder Bay may be colder in winter, less rainy in summer, and lack volcanoes (dormant or otherwise), all three cities seem intent on keeping themselves as tidy as possible, up to a point. And though Puerto Montt may have fewer malls and fast-food outlets, it boasts the largest fish market south of Seattle, as well as the busiest indoor handicraft emporium in central Chile. Here, at the eastern edge of town, in stalls along avenidas Angelmó and Diego Portales, highly skilled artisans display everything from beautiful handknit wool sweaters to ceramics and silver jewelry. The inhabitants are friendly, outgoing, unsuspicious. Though they move a bit more quickly through the streets than the laid-back townsfolk of Ushuaia, they are by no means pushy or frantic. Not like their counterparts in Buenos Aires, New York or Toronto. They make eye contact, smile, say "Hola!" quite willingly. On mild spring afternoons at the end of September, whenever the sun breaks through the overcast and the drizzle lets up, they can be seen enjoying drinks at sidewalk cafés and gazing philosophically out to sea. They eat their evening meals late, stay up well past midnight, roar around on motorcycles. Shrill school kids, colourfully dressed, carry backpacks and umbrellas. Panhandlers are non-existent. Or, if they exist, I didn't see any.

I took an ocean-view room at the Don Luis Gran Hotel, where I was quite comfortable and had a window overlooking Puerto Montt Bay. My first night in town I dined at a nearby restaurant called, for no apparent reason, Balzac, where I feasted on scallops and Chardonnay crab, but passed on the conger eel. I could hear English and German being spoken around me, but very little Spanish.

According to Arturo, the desk clerk at the Don Luis Gran Hotel, there were two obligatory side trips to be made from Puerto Montt. One was by ferry across to the island of Chiloé, ancestral home of the fierce Mapuche tribe and second in size only to Tierra del Fuego. The other would be a lengthy jaunt by motor vessel south along the Chilean fjords, past snowcapped volcanoes and dense forests, to the famous Laguna San Rafael. Here, said Arturo, was where a monstrous blue glacier, inching its way down from Monte San Valentín on the Northern Patagonian icecap, had been calving into the sea for the past several thousand years. An unforgettable, world-class spectacle.

When I asked Arturo which trip he thought I should do, he of course said, "Los dos!" He then summoned his friend Bolívar, the concierge, and inquired about tickets and reservations. According to Bolívar, it would make sense to do the San Rafael Glacier expedition first, followed by a few days on Chiloé, exploring its coastline and three main towns by bus.

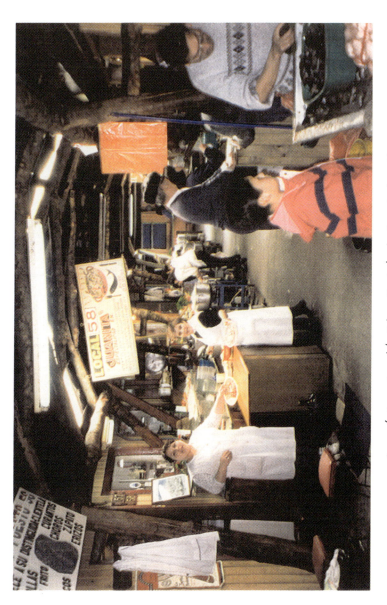

A market on Avenida Diego Portales in Puerto Montt.

That way, he said, I would miss nothing. And could he arrange all these various bookings? Most assuredly. For a modest fee. In an hour, maybe less, depending on the telephone. Was my VISA card in good standing? My American Express? If so, there would be no problem. After all, he had status. He had connections. On the island of Chiloé, in its capital town, Castro, he had an uncle, once removed. Not only that, he was personally acquainted with Captain Alissandro and chief purser Salvador of Skorpios Cruise Lines, whose booking office was just down the street, at the end of avenida Diego Portales. He could, he said, for a small commission, get me the stateroom of my choice. He knew the right people. And talk about timely coincidence! Unless he was mistaken, a nice foreign lady from North America, a school teacher who had checked out of the hotel only the day before, had been asking about that very voyage. What a small world. With luck, and at no extra charge, she could be my traveling companion. For all his help and information, I rewarded Arturo with the largest tip I had yet given since arriving in South America. He seemed genuinely pleased.

And that's how I came to find myself, the following Saturday afternoon, along with sixty other passengers, aboard *Skorpios*, a sleek, speedy, bright orange frigate, built for narrow channels and stormy weather. At first glance, she looked like a streamlined version of the old sub-chasing Corvette. Because of my inability to speak more than a dozen words of Spanish, I was a bit hesitant, but needn't have been. Most of the officers and crew had a smattering of English, as did my fellow adventurers, all of whom, with one notable exception, were from the Chilean towns of Concepción and Valparaíso. Why they were traveling together, in two large groups, I never did discover. I believe they may all have worked for the same software company. At first, I thought the company's name might be Valpo, until I realized that Valpo was what they called Valparaíso for short. The most noticeable thing about these sightseers was that they all wore Rockport shoes and expensive expedition gear, and were festooned with new Nikons. The women sported lots of gold jewelry (it was nice to know that Ponce, Cortés and the boys hadn't grabbed it all), drank gimlets and martinis. The men smoked Cuban cigars and flashed Rolex watches. They were all nicely tanned and took every opportunity to show off their perfect white teeth. And yet, as gregarious and fun-loving as they obviously were, they did not appear phony. Though there was no mistaking their affluence (nary a single commoner from Puerto Montt aboard), it wasn't like being surrounded by egocentric celebrities. Not that I ever have been, but I can imagine. By the same token, they probably assumed that anyone who could afford this voyage had to be well off. The people I conversed with prior to sailing seemed to know where Canada was, though I had the feeling they thought we'd recently been annexed by the U.S.A. Was it true, they wanted to know, that one of our states was preparing to fight for independence, the way they themselves had fought several times against Spain and Peru? If so, they sympathized. They knew that creating a new republic was not easy. One elderly, florid-faced, white-bearded gentleman, wearing a blue plaid shirt and beige fedora, informed me that his nephew in Valparaíso imported Canadian mining equipment and technology. From where, exactly, he wasn't sure, but he thought it might be from the nation's capital, Vancouver. Had I ever been there? Well, so had he. Ten years ago. Not with his wife, but with her sister. Whatever that meant. And just what line of work was I in? I didn't look like a lawyer, physician or industrialist. An anthropologist, perhaps? A scientific writer? None of the above, I said, and left it at that.

The other non-Chilean on board, the one Bolívar had mentioned, turned out to be a very pleasant, middle-aged, elementary school teacher from Ottawa. She was on sabbatical leave and her name was Catherine. I discovered her on the sun deck just prior to sailing. She was sitting by herself, out of the wind, gazing down at the flurry of activity on the pier. Cases of wine were being trundled aboard. Latecomers came scurrying up the gangway. Crew members were saying good-bye to loved ones. Boys were hawking week-old newspapers without much success. I introduced myself to Catherine, said I was happy to find another English-speaking passenger. How incredibly coincidental that halfway around the world, two itinerant Ontarians should meet on a Chilean boat. Nor did the coincidence end there: like her, I too was on sabbatical leave. Not from elementary school, but from the English department of a large, inner city high school.

"But you do speak Spanish?" Catherine said, raising her coat collar against the damp breeze, pulling an unusual embroidered hat, like a tarboosh without the tassel, over her brown hair.

"No," I said. "I'm afraid I don't. I wish I'd studied it at university."

She laughed. "I wish I had too. All I could manage was French, and that just barely. I can't believe I'm here in South America as a unilingual tourist. That's what comes from spur of the moment travel plans. Or lack thereof. I'd be interested to know what brings a fellow Canadian teacher all the way to Chile."

Just then *Skorpios* blew her whistle and we could detect the increased rumble of her engines down below. Lines were being cast off. People on shore were shouting. Slowly, we eased stern-first away from the wharf and backed out into Puerto Montt Bay. The wind freshened, raindrops fell. "I was on my way north from Ushuaia," I said, "intending to finish up back in Buenos Aires. When I got to Bariloche, people said, 'You really must check out the lake district of Chile, see some glaciers and volcanoes.' So here I am. And you?"

Catherine smiled, shook her head. She was wearing a jade necklace that caught the light and matched her eyes perfect-ly. "Nothing quite so logical. I couldn't stand the crowds and congestion in Santiago, so I bought a train ticket to the southern terminus of the railroad. Which happened to be Puerto Montt."

"So you're not on a planned itinerary?"

Again she laughed, in a sardonic, unaffected way, as though genuinely amused at what I'd said. "Hardly. All I'm doing is running to escape. Tell me about Ushuaia. I may go there next. Either that or Punta Arenas."

Several people came up and joined us, stood at the rail waving and snapping photographs of Puerto Montt harbour. I debated telling Catherine my real reason for visiting Ushuaia, decided against it. Two agile young waiters in uniform came bounding up the stairs with trays of drinks and hors d'oeuvres. They seemed to think we should go down below out of the weather, shook their heads in disbelief when we indicated we'd prefer to stay topside. I didn't know it at the time, but this was the start of what was to be a nonstop barrage of free booze and appetizers during the voyage, offered frequently, almost forcibly.

"Ushuaia," I said, "is truly the end of the earth. It's bleak and desolate, like Baffin Island."

Catherine raised a glass, sipped it, smacked her lips. "Well, I've never been to Baffin Island. Actually, I'm not that fussy about islands in general, unless they're the size of Newfoundland. A little hangup I have. So tell me, is Ushuaia worth a visit or not? My guide book is noncommittal."

"Depends on what you're running from," I said, sipping my own drink, which tasted strongly of rum.

"If you must know," Catherine said, throwing canapés by the handful to a squadron of following gulls, "I'm running from a sordid, sticky divorce. My idea was to get as far away from home as possible. Breathe some fresh air, see new faces, consort with foreigners. I figured Patagonia should do the trick. If the waiters on this boat keep the libations coming, I may just emerge unscathed. So far, it's been nip and tuck. What are your table arrangements at mealtime, by the way?"

I'd been wondering the same thing. "I imagine I'll be at a table full of Chileans."

"In view of the language barrier, I made the bold move of reserving the last table for two. Probably a mistake. Bound to be misinterpreted. Not that I'm standoffish, or have anything

Señor Ibañez.

against being exposed to Spanish, but under the circumstances ..."

"You'd rather sit by yourself?"

"No, I'd rather have company. But not the strain of trying to make myself understood. I've about had my fill of that
lately. I don't suppose you'd consider joining my enclave
against the conquistadores?"

"I would indeed," I said. "In fact, I'd like it very much. I
can't believe my good fortune. As for your divorce, I can
empathize, but not sympathize with you. I went through the
same thing five years ago, though mine wasn't sordid.
Unpleasant and deflating, but not sordid. It just had to be
done. People understood. My lawyer told me to think of it as
using whiteout on a page of bad writing. So if you won't talk
about yours, I won't talk about mine."

We clinked glasses to seal the bargain, tossed off our
drinks, took fresh ones from the tray. More and more people
were coming up on deck to watch the shoreline recede. They
all carried cocktails, all said, "Buenas tardes!" They stood at
the stern rail, photographing each other and laughing.
Catherine and I exchanged glances. The bearded man in the
beige fedora, with binoculars hanging round his neck,
approached us and introduced himself as señor Ibañez. He
said he was a widower, travelling alone. He pointed across the
water at the misty shores of a steep-sided island. "Chiloé," he
said reverently. "Eez ber' nice, ber' history. You should bisit
these island."

Catherine nodded, turned to me. "Have you been there?"

"I was planning to do it after the voyage."

"So was I. Apparently the Chilotes wanted independence
not only from Spain, but from Peru and Chile too. You have
to hand it to them. They knew what would make them happy
and went after it. I'm still in the process of adjusting to independence myself."

It took us four days of leisurely sailing to reach Laguna San
Rafael and its massive blue glacier. We stopped at isolated

fishing ports along the way, poked our nose into densely-forested fjords where the coastal Andes rose starkly out of the Pacific. There was still snow on the higher peaks, and señor Ibañez, always in his beige fedora, knew the names of all the volcanoes, the dates of all the earthquakes. He appointed himself our personal tour guide, took it upon himself to translate into fractured English the announcements booming over the loudspeakers at frequent intervals.

On the second day, as we made our way slowly up a deep, narrow inlet, with snowcapped pinnacles towering over us, we were told that in 1834, Charles Darwin had entered here, vainly seeking a short cut through the mountains to Argentina. Cruising east along this very channel, he thought he'd found it. All on board the *Beagle* had celebrated. But sadly, like the French explorers of Canada bound for China via the mighty St. Lawrence, Darwin and his mates were doomed to disappointment. They eventually came to a stone wall. There was no shortcut. The only route to Argentina, unless you were a surefooted vicuña, was around treacherous Cape Horn.

Next morning under drizzly skies we meandered among the bleak Islas Hichlas of the Puyuhaupi Archipelago. Señor Ibañez informed us that not until 1900, four centuries after the beginning of Spanish colonization, did the Chilean government finally send mapmakers to this end of the country. Before that, no one knew what was here. The only inhabitants were fierce tribes of Guaeticas Indians, and they were few and far between.

In the afternoon we reached the remote fishing village of Puerto Aguirre and tied up at a rickety pier in a protected little bay. All the villagers, forty or fifty of them, came down to greet us. They brought their children along too, and though Catherine and I didn't comprehend at first, the idea was that the children would act as guides for those *Skorpios* passengers wishing to disembark and tour the village. Señor Ibañez said that though the elders would not allow these child-guides to accept currency in payment for their services, it was permissible to reward them with gifts of paper, pens, books, fruit or candy. The little wooden church, he said, was worth seeing, and the small cemetery, in which graves dated all the way back to 1830, when Chile had been in conflict with Peru and rebels had come down the coast looking for the murderers of presidential-aide Diego Palazuelos. Señor Ibañez also recommended visiting certain shingle-covered houses along the shore in which the women of Puerto Aguirre had their looms and wove the finest wool garments in all of Chile.

Braving wind and drizzle, Catherine and I stepped ashore under umbrellas. But by the time we arrived at the staging point for the guided tours, all the children had been spoken for. All save one, that is, who told us her name was Lucia.

Lucia was a dark-complexioned little girl of eight or nine, with straight black hair and luminous eyes. She was wearing a purple jacket. The first thing you noticed about her was that she had a severe limp. It might have been due to a birth defect, or because one leg was shorter than the other. She appeared eager to guide us, though, stood up and approached us. But just then an older woman, perhaps her mother or her aunt, very shabbily dressed, intervened. She shook her head, rattled at us in Spanish, pointed at herself. It was an awkward situation. Little Lucia, retreating, was obviously crushed by the woman's intervention. She sat down on a stone with her back turned, refusing to look at us. From the way her shoulders trembled, I assumed she was crying. The thought crossed my mind that this might be a clever scam. That Lucia was faking her deformity and her accomplice saw us as easy marks for sympathetic handouts. As I was thinking this, señor Ibañez came along, holding an umbrella over his head. His shiny brown shoes were in danger of losing their lustre to mud. He said he had no desire to tour the village, that his walking days were over. He was only stretching his muscles. Noticing Lucia, he told us she represented a mixture of Mapuche and Spanish blood, which, in the right proportions, could produce attractive features. In the wrong proportions, he said, results might vary. After speaking to Lucia's guardian,

Lucia, child guide at Puerto Aguirre.

Catherine at Puerto Aguirre.

he told us that the child was not really a guide at all, because of her disability. Though she came down to meet boats with the other children, it was obvious she couldn't very well lead tourists about the village. Not in a satisfactory manner.

By this time, the other passengers were far away, up near the church, wandering among the weather-beaten houses. We could see them walking in little groups behind their diminutive leaders, stopping to take pictures. Catherine surprised me then, by asking señor Ibañez to inform the woman that as we were in no hurry, we wanted Lucia as our guide and no one else. At first, I thought the woman was going to refuse. She even appeared a little angry. Señor Ibañez said to us, "There is embarrassment that the girl cannot keep up and show you the sights. If you care to wait, another guide will be sent for."

"We don't want another guide," Catherine said sternly, showing her stubborn, feisty side, walking over to Lucia and placing a hand on her shoulder. "We want this one."

It was an interesting moment. I imagined Catherine in divorce court, stating her case. I imagined her in a classroom, maintaining order with gentle insistence. The rain had stopped and a few elderly villagers had strolled over to see what we were doing. Up on its hill, the church bell suddenly clanged. Across the bay, smoke from scattered dwellings rose into the damp air. I waved at those passengers on board *Skorpios* who had elected not to come ashore and were standing on deck with drinks in their hands. The next thing I knew, Catherine had taken Lucia by the hand and the two of them were starting off along a muddy track toward the nearest houses. I saw now that Lucia's limp was not faked. She really did have trouble walking. Though at first it was painful to watch as she heaved herself along, you couldn't help but admire her courage. Holding Catherine's hand tightly, using it for support, she pointed out the sights and prattled away in Spanish, as though her spiel, though seldom if ever used, had been well rehearsed. She stopped every so often to rest and catch her breath, and Catherine would ask her lengthy questions in English. This had the effect of making the two of them giggle like schoolgirls. As I followed along behind, I had the impression of watching a skit, in which the actors shared some kind of secret, unintelligible joke. The fact that they couldn't understand each other apparently had no effect whatsoever on their enjoyment of the outing. Holding hands, they trudged slowly but determinedly on. They would take turns pointing, nod their heads, take a few steps and stop. A scrawny orange cat emerged from a clump of bushes and accompanied them for a short distance, then charged off after a low-flying bird.

One thing about this walking tour—we had lots of time to look around. Not only that, though our progress was slow and halting, and though we didn't get anywhere near the church or the weavers and potters that everyone else talked about back on board, we did eventually put some distance between us and the ship. It was a curious feeling, being in this remote fishing village so far from civilization, unable to speak the language, yet communicating quite well with a child of Mapuche and Spanish descent. At one point, as Catherine and Lucia forged ahead, I found myself standing alone in the middle of the road, listening to the sigh of the wind and the splashing of waves against the beach. I suddenly realized I was a long way from home. In the distance, *Skorpios*, tied to her dock, looked almost too small to be real. I was surprised at how far we'd walked. The sun had lost its battle with the clouds and drizzle was falling again. Up at the church, you could hear children's shrill voices. When I looked for Catherine and Lucia, I saw them coming back toward me, still hand in hand, still deep in conversation. Walking downhill, Lucia was having just as much difficulty as she'd had going up, but when Catherine, with gestures, offered to carry her piggyback, she shook her head vigorously, seeming to say, "Tour guides do not accept rides from clients."

Of course we were the last ones to reach the dock. By then, most of the other children had dispersed, running off home with the loot they'd acquired from yet another influx of big city tourists. We saw a few youngsters carrying pads of

Patricio and Catherine aboard Skorpios.

writing paper, pencils with erasers, boxes of crayons. Of course what you were supposed to have done, what everybody else did, was stop at the little store beside the church and purchase suitable items for your guide. The only trouble was, we hadn't gone anywhere near the church, which stood aloof on its hill overlooking the harbour. And so as our tour ended, we suddenly realized that we had nothing to give Lucia. I searched my pockets, came up with nothing but three 500 peso banknotes and a handful of 10 peso coins. In any event, cash had been expressly forbidden. It was an awkward moment, a sad moment. Lucia stood there expectantly, not with her hand out, but obviously hoping to be rewarded, just as all the other tour guides had been. The fact that she'd seen her peers laden with goodies didn't help matters. So Catherine did a marvelous thing. She reached into her handbag, took out a beautiful gold retractable ballpoint pen, and gave it to Lucia. Then she took off her jade necklace (which she said later was not expensive, but I somehow think it was) and placed it around the child's neck. Lucia held the gold pen in her hand, admiring it, turning it over in her fingers, eyes wide with delight. Then she touched the necklace, and though she couldn't see much of it, seemed to realize it was special. For the first time all afternoon she stopped talking. She stood there in the drizzle, black hair shining, holding the pen in one hand, touching the jade necklace with the other. On her dark, young face was a look of pleasure, of gratitude, of friendship. A pair of old women who had been watching, nodded, clucked their tongues approvingly. I had the feeling that Lucia would gladly have guided us for free, that being pressed into service was reward enough, but at the same time, Catherine's gifts had left her speechless. When I looked toward *Skorpios*, I saw our shipmates standing at the stern rail, watching us. Deckhands were ready to cast off lines. Captain Alissandro was in his wheelhouse. No one looked impatient, yet it was obviously time to go. Rain was coming down harder, cool gusts of wind ruffled the bay. Catherine knelt, took Lucia in her arms, gave her a tremendous hug. They both had tears in their eyes, like old friends parting. Up on the sun deck I heard a smattering of applause.

What I remember from that day at Puerto Aguirre isn't the wooden church or the looms or the pottery, but the sight of a little handicapped girl in a purple coat standing in the rain, waving at us as we pulled away from the wharf and headed for Pilcomayo Channel under a darkening sky. Southward, in the far distance, rose the sheer, misty mountains of the Patagonian coast range.

In the snug lounge on Acropolis deck, Patricio, our favourite waiter, brought us mugs of spicy, mulled Chicureo. It was a good place to be on a late September afternoon, sailing southward, surrounded by people speaking a foreign tongue. Señor Ibañez came and joined us, and out of the blue Catherine asked him to talk about the regimes and legacies of Salvador Allende, Augusto Pinochet and Eduardo Frie. Señor Ibañez looked at her with alarm, glanced about the room, put his finger to his lips. He shook his head, raised his hands like a traffic policeman. "No, señora," he said. "It would be a bad thing. You should not ask me that. You should not ask any Chilean that. Many Chileans died. This is too sad, too violent to talk about."

* * *

Chapter 4.

From Puerto Aguirre to Laguna San Rafael, by way of Quitralco Fjord and Ferronave Channel. Then north up Golfo Corcovado to Puerto Montt.

According to Catherine's guide book, the spring-fed thermal pools of Quitralco Island, south of Puerto Aguirre, have been in use for hundreds of years. Supposedly, Charles Darwin and Captain FitzRoy, of HMS *Beagle*, enjoyed a relaxing dip there while cataloguing condors. Peruvian pirates from Lima also extolled the steamy vapours. If dispatches back to Holland from prowling corsairs can be believed, even Dutch sailors stopped briefly and soaked themselves prior to 1600.

At breakfast on the chilly morning of our arrival, señor Ibañez gave a scientific explanation for the pools' existence, which I did not fully grasp. He theorized that heated subterranean streams from Volcán Hudson on the mainland, due west of us, percolated up through the rocks of Quitralco Fjord. However, at dinner that evening, during which we were guests of honour at Captain Alissandro's table, chief purser Salvador scoffed at the idea of hot water coming all the way from Volcán Hudson. "Is no possible," he said. "Is too far for these water." Neither he nor Captain Alissandro, however, could offer a more feasible scenario.

We went ashore in bright orange lifeboats. Though it was foggy and spitting rain, everyone was upbeat. To celebrate the midpoint of our voyage, we'd had champagne in our breakfast orange juice. Many of us took along our towels and bathing suits, and as soon as we had disembarked, the boats went back out to *Skorpios* for pastries and urns of hot coffee sweetened with rum.

I must say, it was extraordinarily pleasant, wallowing about in these bubbling, steaming pools of hot water, with

Going ashore at Quitralco.

Catherine and Skorpios at Quitralco.

cool drizzle falling on your head and a tangy breeze blowing in off the fjord. I was surprised at how many of the Chilean passengers jumped in, intent on frolicking. Some of them lay back and soaked, others began singing. Catherine, I noticed, without knowing the words, sang along too, faking it. This pleased everyone, and she received compliments on her voice. It was like being in a Jacuzzi full of tipsy, friendly strangers. Every known body shape and degree of hairiness was represented, yet there was not a hint of embarrassment. Several members of the dining room staff, including our favourite waiter, Patricio, hovered near us, keeping us supplied with rum-laced coffee and iced drinks.

Sometime during the morning, just as at Puerto Aguirre, I sat back and thought how bizarre this was—sitting in a coastal hot tub in the wilds of Patagonia, miles from civilization, being splashed good-naturedly by people I barely knew. People of another culture, whose language I didn't speak. There was something surreal, too, about strait-laced Patricio running around under an umbrella, handing drinks to people in bathing suits. As noon approached, and we showed no signs of emerging, lifeboats were sent back to the ship for wine and sandwiches. The wind was quite chilly now, the rain more intense, and we became totally enveloped in swirling vapours. To keep warm, you had to stay submerged, with the result that we all began to look like boiled lobsters. Was it my imagination, or was there a degree of surreptitious groping going on? It was hard to tell, but judging from the women's squeals, I suspect there was.

Finally, at two o'clock, Captain Alissandro blew his whistle and our chaperones informed us it was time to leave, if we were to reach Laguna San Rafael before dark. We crawled reluctantly out of the pools, changed into our clothes in one of two large tents, and were ferried back out to *Skorpios*, where a hot lunch of *curanto* was waiting.

It was at this rather raucous meal that Catherine and I found ourselves at a table for eight, surrounded by Chileans. When we asked Patricio what had happened to our cozy table for two, he said that purser Salvador, acting on a suggestion from Captain Alissandro, had removed it from the dining room. "For these companerismo," he said. "For these diálogo."

All afternoon, under scudding clouds, we bore southward in Farronave Channel, skirting wild-looking islands, with now and then a glimpse of open ocean off to starboard. On our port side, mountains rose abruptly out of the sea and soared skyward. Occasionally, there were waterfalls and small glaciers, which señor Ibañez referred to as "ventisqueros." The beaches we passed were deserted. There was no habitation, no chimney smoke, no sign of life. We saw no boats and very few sea birds. At tea time, one of the younger female passengers came in, red-cheeked, and said she'd seen a whale. No one seemed interested. They may not have believed her. Catherine and I put on sweaters and jackets, and, standing at the bow of the ship, thought we saw a whale too. Either that or a dolphin. Or possibly an otter, or a dark wave.

Laguna San Rafael is really a long, finger-shaped bay. It's neither a lake nor a lagoon. Dense stands of tall alerce trees cover the foothills of its eastern shore, with craggy, brooding mountains rising steeply above. Westward, it is separated from the Pacific by the desolate Taitao Peninsula. If this peninsula, jutting out from shore like the Rock of Gibraltar, were an island, then Laguna San Rafael would be a narrow channel and you could continue sailing southward to lower Patagonia. But it's not a channel, so you can't. You're in a cul-de-sac. Your way is solidly blocked. You've no choice but to turn around and retrace your steps.

We entered Laguna San Rafael from the north at dusk and spent the night an anchor. In the morning, the first thing we saw was the mind-blowing turquoise glacier, facing us across a kilometre or two of calm water. I understood immediately why this was the highlight of the trip, and why things had been timed so that we'd be here at first light. The early sun made the glacier sparkle like stained glass, as though illuminated from within. Icebergs surrounded us, some big,

The author at the San Rafael glacier.

Iceberg from the glacier in Laguna San Rafael.

some tiny, but all with a strange cobalt luminescence. I'll admit we were awestruck. Sixty of us stood silently, reverently, at the port rail. A few people snapped pictures, or, like señor Ibañez, looked through binoculars, but most of us, including the deck officers, who must have witnessed this many times, just stood and stared. Without warning, a massive slab of blue ice detached itself from high up on the glacier's frontal wall and fell into the sea, making a tremendous splash. Seconds later, we heard the sound. Among us, there were moans, gasps of wonder. No actual words, just a long, drawn-out "Ahhhhhhhh," like a chorus, or restrained orgasm. As the fallen slab of ice bobbed to the surface, rolling and pitching, its minor tidal wave reached us, of sufficient strength to rock the ship a little. Every ten or fifteen minutes after that, a similar piece of ice would break off and fall, making you realize that this was in fact a congealed, slowly moving river.

Señor Ibañez, who, while knowledgeable, was becoming a bit of a pest, took it upon himself to inform us that the San Rafael glacier was 45 kilometres long, over 70 metres deep, and that its face measured three kilometres across. Perhaps because we didn't seem sufficiently impressed, he added that it was 30,000 years old and on an average day disgorged two million cubic metres of ice into the lagoon. Which, he said, would explain the profusion of floating icebergs. Where he got his numbers from, I'm not sure. We never saw him with a guide book in his hand, so maybe he made them up. That morning, I wished he would be quiet. It wasn't a time for facts and figures, but rather for looking, for admiring. I didn't really care how long or how deep the glacier was. Had we been contemplating the sphinx, I would not have wanted someone nattering at me about its estimated age, or how long it was, or who built it. Maybe later, but not now. I was beginning to see why his countrymen tended to ignore señor Ibañez, and why he'd attached himself to us. Catherine made the comment that every tour, every excursion, seemed to have its señor Ibañez.

After breakfast, with the ship still anchored, those of us who wanted to were invited to clamber into the orange lifeboats and go in closer to the glacier. This, said purser Salvador, would give us a better chance to gauge its height and photograph it from sea level. The only thing was, if it calved a large block while we were in front of it, we might get bounced around by the surge. But not to worry, our boatman, whoever it might be, would have experience in such circumstances. What purser Salvador didn't tell us, so as not to spoil the surprise, was that on board the lifeboats would be bottles of twelve-year-old Scotch whiskey, which we would chill in our glasses with bits of thirty-thousand-year-old ice chipped from a floating berg. To everyone's relief, señor Ibañez elected to stay on board and await our return. He said he'd seen more than his share of glaciers, had drunk more than his share of twelve-year-old Scotch. "Make sure there's no hair in these ice cube," he warned, referring perhaps to the recently reported discovery of a frozen milodon carcass in the Northern Patagonian ice-cap.

We set sail that evening during dinner, shaping a northerly course toward Río Tempanos and the Herrera Islands. Heading in this direction, we had spectacular mountains to starboard for a change, and Pérez Norte Channel to port. After dinner we had a program of Chilean folksongs in the lounge, performed by a group of ladies from Valparaíso. To my utter amazement, when purser Salvador, acting as master of ceremonies, asked Catherine to sing a Canadian folksong, she stood up and led the entire room in a rousing rendition of *Alouette*, complete with hand gestures. For an encore she sang *Un Canadien Errant*, which everyone said sounded very mournful, very sad. Patricio was kept busy bringing drinks to restore happiness.

We sailed all that night, and next morning found ourselves anchored at the eastern end of a narrow inlet on the mainland, opposite the small coastal hamlet of Puerto Chacabuco. We were told that our original destination had been

Aboard Skorpios, in the Chilean fjords.

Puerto Aisén, a larger, more interesting settlement, but unfortunately, Puerto Aisén's harbour had become so silted up that *Skorpios* could not enter. The reason for the silt, if you can believe señor Ibañez, is that too many trees have been logged or burned off the hillsides, so now the soil runs down into the sea unimpeded. This may or may not be true. We were also told that the jagged, snowcapped mountain peaks surrounding us, many with small glaciers, give the region the exact appearance of Alaska. Off in the distance, but clearly visible, stood the Volcán Cóndor, rearing its head above the clouds. Señor Ibañez said that the Cóndor had blown its stack several times in the past, and might be getting ready to do so again.

A number of Concepción passengers, disappointed at not being able to reach Puerto Aisén, where the longest suspension bridge in Latin America supposedly resides, wanted to go ashore at Puerto Chacabuco instead. I'm not sure what attracted them, other than an old church and some shops, and perhaps the chance to mail postcards. To me, what made it worthwhile, even without going ashore, was the sight of snowcapped glacial mountains plunging straight down into the fjord.

In any event, no one left the ship. It seems heavy weather was brewing to the west, out beyond the Archipiélago de los Chonos, and so Captain Alissandro deemed it advisable to scurry northward and seek shelter behind Isla Magdalena. This we did, and found smooth sailing all the way into Puerto Puyuhuapi, at the foot of Mount Melimoyu. Here, coincidentally, purser Salvador's sister and brother-in-law managed the luxurious Puyuhuapi Hotel and Spa.

We anchored at suppertime in a deep, quiet cove frequented by cormorants. After a stroll about the deck, señor Ibañez came in for cocktails and said he'd seen a family of black necked swans. As with the girl who said she'd seen a whale, people tended to disbelieve him. Speaking of señor Ibañez, ever since Catherine and I had been moved to a table for eight, he'd insisted on sitting with us, either beside Catherine or beside me. On this occasion, he positioned himself between us and talked non-stop. And so before dessert, we got up and left him there. We joined a small group of people going ashore for the evening, and ended up at the posh Puyuhuapi Hotel and Spa, which Catherine said reminded her of Fantasy Island. We drank potent pisco sours in a beautiful dining room overlooking the cove, but turned down

Skorpios in the Chilean fjords near Archipiélago de la Chonos.

offers to be wrapped in warm seaweed and massaged. Unlike the thermal pools at Quitralco, which had been quaintly primitive, these at Puyuhuapi were very elegant. Attendants were eager to fuss over you. The seawater hot tubs did indeed look inviting. Purser Salvador's sister said that if we were to stay a few days, we would be treated to the finest food and accommodation in all of Chile. At no extra charge, a visit to the famous Puyuhuapi carpet factory would be included.

It was midnight before we returned to the ship. Catherine and I sat out under the stars for an hour, talking, sipping chilled Chardonnay from the Cousiño-Macul winery in Santiago. It occurred to us that the voyage was rapidly drawing to a close. Another day of sailing north up the Golfo Corcovado, with brief stops to view the volcanoes Nevado and Chaitén, and then we'd be back in Puerto Montt, our starting point. I asked Catherine if she'd come to any decision regarding her plans after that, and she said no, she hadn't.

I did not know until next morning at breakfast that she did indeed have plans. When I sat down at my usual place, Patricio handed me a note from her. Before I read it, he informed me she'd left the ship at dawn, an hour before sailing, had taken her luggage ashore, and was planning to spend a few days at the Puyuhuapi Hotel and Spa. Which was pretty well what her note said: "Nothing personal, but I need some peace and quiet and time to think. As I'm not one for roughing it, this looks like the perfect place. Purser Salvador phoned his sister for me to see if she had a vacant room. All she had was a suite, which will be a nice change from my *Skorpios* cabin, and comes complete with massages and mud packs. I've been seeking just such a Shangri-la for ages, but never expected to find one so far from home. I hope we can rendezvous in the not too distant future, perhaps when you're finished in Puerto Montt and I'm finished whirlpooling. I understand the Patagonia Express people have a ferryboat that goes three times a week from here to Quellón on Chiloé Island. I'll probably take it next Friday, then go by bus to Castro. They also do trips down to the San Rafael glacier, but as I've already done that aboard *Skorpios*, I believe I'll pass. Anyway, I've tentatively booked a room in Castro at the Hostería Unicornio Azul, which they tell me has a nice view of the harbour and isn't too expensive. I'd be pleased if our paths crossed. Forgive my sudden, unplanned, unannounced departure, but I tend to be a spur of the moment type person lately. Call it survival instinct. I'd also had my fill of señor Ibañez. It was either jump ship this morning or throw him overboard. I beg your indulgence. Hoping to see you on Chiloé, Catherine."

We charged north at full speed, with the wind on our port beam and the decks wet with spray. It began to rain right after breakfast, and until we gained the protection of the Archipiélago de los Guaitecas south of Chiloé, we took the cresting waves broadside. Passengers either stayed in the lounge drinking pisco or retreated to their cabins. To escape señor Ibañez, who was following me like a puppy, demanding to know what I'd done to offend Catherine, I went out on deck and found a sheltered spot behind the starboard lifeboats. From there, through the rain, I had a misty view of mainland mountains, and was surprised at the number of volcanoes. Had they all decided to erupt at once, it would have been impressive. Finally, when I was thoroughly chilled and tired of the ship's rolling, I went in and spent an hour updating my journal. I also pricked my thumb and took a blood-sugar reading, which I hadn't done in some time, and was chagrined to find it alarmingly high. Big meals, too much wine and too many cocktails were taking their toll. Resolving to cut back, yet knowing how weak I was, I prepared for the Captain's gala farewell dinner by doubling my midday dose of insulin.

As we drew in behind Chiloé and got some protection from the Pacific swells, the ship settled down and I slept the entire afternoon. I had a ridiculous dream of Catherine, in which she, Captain Alissandro and señor Ibañez were all sitting on a sparkling white veranda, their faces and torsos covered with black mud. Until they spoke and called me by name, I didn't recognize them.

When we sat down to Captain Alissandro's farewell dinner, of course señor Ibañez placed himself next to me. During toasts and speeches by purser Salvador, Ibañez said how disappointed he was that Catherine was not there to join the celebration. He said he had a gift for her, a white wool hat with the word *Skorpios* stitched along the side. He said he'd bought it on board, with the idea of presenting it to her at the farewell dinner. While he spoke, I tried to recall where I'd seen such a hat, and suddenly remembered—Maria Malaspina had been wearing one in Ushuaia. I told señor Ibañez that I would likely see Catherine on Chiloé in a few days' time, and could give her the hat then. But for reasons best known to himself, he declined my offer. He may not have believed me, may have held me responsible for her departure. He said, "My wife run away too. Many times. But now she not run away no more. Now I run away. I like to run away on these boat."

For the next half hour, while officers, cooks and waiters were being introduced and applauded, he told me in excruciating detail everything he knew about Volcán Hornopirén, dimly visible off our starboard quarter. He said there was a town of the same name, a town he knew well, on the Golfo de Ancud, where he and his dear, departed wife had once honeymooned. "You know what is these honeymoon?" he said, winking lewdly. "These luna de miel? I think you don' know these."

We docked at Puerto Montt under a rising moon, but were allowed to stay in our cabins till morning if we wished. Some people stayed, others departed. A line of taxis whisked crew members away. I should have said goodbye to Captain Alissandro and purser Salvador and everyone else who had been so kind during the voyage. I should have put money in the envelopes provided and handed them personally to Reina, my chambermaid, and to Patricio, my favourite waiter. I should have gone and said goodbye to señor Ibañez, who, despite his verbosity, had meant well. But I did none of those things. Instead, I locked myself in my cabin, swigged an unhealthy nightcap of Chicureo red, and slept fitfully till six a.m., at which time I showered, packed and went in search of a taxi to take me back to the Hotel Don Luis. The last view I had of the good ship *Skorpios*, my floating home for so many pleasant days, was as a watery sun rose behind her out of Puerto Montt Bay, at the end of avenida Diego Portales. Despite the early hour, there was activity along the quay. Down at the fish market, boats were coming in. Men and women were bustling about the wharves, drinking coffee, talking. As I stood waiting for a cab, I was very glad I'd made the trip to Laguna San Rafael, but still, it felt good to be ashore.

* * *

Chapter 5.

On the Island of Chiloé—
"Land of the Andean Gull."

"The island of Chiloé is celebrated for its black storms
and black soil, its thickets of fuchsia and bamboo, its
Jesuit churches and the golden hands of its wood-
carvers. Among its shellfish there is an enormous bar-
nacle—the pico de mar—which sits on one's plate like
a miniature Mount Fugi."
　　　　—Bruce Chatwin: *What Am I Doing Here.*

Guide books disagree on the exact size of Chiloé. Some give
its length as 180 km, others as much as 250 km. I suppose it
depends where you measure from. There appears to be less
disagreement as to its width—between 50 and 60 km. The
way I see it, Chiloé is twice as long and twice as wide as Lake
Superior's Isle Royale. Which is to say, half as long and half as
wide as Vancouver Island. It's also much closer to the nearest
mainland shore than either Isle Royale or Vancouver Island—
less than 3 kilometres. And yet, there's no bridge to Chiloé,
just as there's no bridge to Isle Royale or Vancouver Island.
There's no airport, either. There is, however, a north-south
highway and a bunch of minor roads. There are big trees, big
cliffs, a plethora of sand and rocky beaches, especially on the
wild western side. There are three fair-sized towns of over
20,000: Ancud, in the north, Castro (the capital) in the middle, and Quellón in the south. There are also half a dozen
smaller settlements and quite a few coastal villages. A lot of
Chiloé is taken up by forest and two national parks: Parque
Nacional Chepu in the north, Parque Nacional Anay in the
south. In summer (our winter) these parks are open to

campers and backpackers. In winter (our summer) they're closed. When I was there at the end of September (early spring), there were a few tourists, but not many. None that I encountered had ever been to Canada.

The original inhabitants of Chiloé, called *Chilotes*, were seafaring Mapuche and Chonos Indians from Patagonia. When the Spaniards arrived in the mid-1500's, they killed off many of the natives with various epidemics, then enslaved the rest. Because of its isolation and defensibility, Chiloé was pretty well the last Spanish stronghold in South America during the Chilean struggle for independence. Regular mainland uprisings were staged and battles fought, but not until 1826 was the last Spaniard driven off Chiloé and complete independence proclaimed. This was nothing new, of course. Argentina had already done it to Spain, Brazil to Portugal, the United States to England. So far, keep your fingers crossed, Canada hasn't needed to do it to anyone.

Mind you, vestiges of Spanish influence are still very prevalent on Chiloé: language, facial features, the Catholic religion (150 wooden churches, built by the Jesuits, dot the island). In recent times, at least since 1960, when an earthquake reshaped the coastline and shook down all the *palafitos* (dwellings built out over the water on pilings), things have been pretty stable. The inhabitants appear to be frugal, honest and hard working—qualities which stand them in good stead when they go abroad to seek employment. As with Newfoundlanders, though, young people tend to flee the island for opportunities elsewhere. They go north to Santiago, Valparaíso, La Serena, some even as far as Peru and Argentina.

My original plan was to take a Cruz del Sur bus to the ferry terminal at Pargua, 55 km southwest of Puerto Montt. From there, I'd make the twenty minute crossing to the village of Chacao on Chiloé's northeast tip, board a second bus, and proceed south to Castro. The only drawback was that I would miss visiting the town of Ancud, which señor Ibañez had said was a must-see, because of its Chilote museum and rusty old Spanish cannons. So I asked Arturo, the desk clerk at the Hotel Don Luis, if there was another way, and he said yes, there was. What I should do, according to him, was allow his brothers, Cervantes and Manuel, who ran a daily ferry service between Puerto Montt and Ancud, to take me with them aboard their boat, the *Maritza del Carmen*. By claiming me as a personal friend, Arturo said he might even persuade his brothers to offer a small discount on the fare, which was 4000 pesos, or ten American dollars. "Eez much better," he said. "You no hab these bus to Pargua, you no hab these barca de pasaje to Chacao. Eez much better you go my brothers on these *Maritza del Carmen*. Ber' nice, ber' safe. You hab no problem, señor."

I then asked him if he knew of a decent hotel in Ancud, and he said yes, he did, the Galeón Azul, on the site of the old Spanish fort, Fuerte San Antonio, overlooking Ancud harbour. "Eez ber' nice, señor. No cheap, no expenses. For you, eez jus' right. Eez manage by my cousin, Ramón."

For the second time in our short relationship, I gave Arturo an excessively large tip. Not just as reward for services rendered, but because I liked him and had a sneaking suspicion I might need him again someday. I've found that when travelling, such tips are a sound investment. Better than insurance.

Next day, after a morning spent wandering the length of avenida Diego Portales, looking in shop windows, staring and being stared at, I boarded the wooden-hulled, turquoise-trimmed Maritza del Carmen. Pocketing my fare, Cervantes, who acted as purser while Manuel steered, advised me that the trip might take as little as four hours, depending on whether or not we stopped at Calbuco to pick up passengers.

In fact, we didn't stop, and it was a calm, pleasant voyage, under bright sun, in the company of a dozen smiling Chilotes. Among them were two teenage sisters, Matilde and Enricheta, on their way home to the fishing village of Caulín, where the oldest church and the best oysters in all of Chile

Sisters, Matilde and Enricheta.

The Maritza del Carmen of Manuel and Cervantes.

were found, and which I gathered was not far from Ancud. The girls were studying English in school, they said, and hoped one day to go and live in Santiago with their aunt, who was a nurse. They had been to Puerto Montt to visit an older, married sister, and to make arrangements for starting high school next semester. Their father, they said, an oyster fisherman, would be at Ancud to meet them in his boat. And yes, they had a vague idea where Canada was—somewhere near the Arctic Circle, where polar bears lived. Did we really have polar bears? Certainly. And pingüinos? No, not penguins. What a pity. Chile had pingüinos. Magellanic pingüinos. Not as many as Argentina, but enough. Why was English so hard to learn? Sometimes their teacher threw up her hands and called them stupid. Why didn't everyone learn Spanish, a prettier, easier language?

At mid-voyage, surprisingly (to me, at least), Cervantes served steaming bowls of oyster chowder in the cabin, accompanied by beer, fresh oysters and fried potato dumplings, which I believe he called *chapaleles*. As I was finishing my second beer, he came around and tried to collect 500 pesos from everyone. I noticed that some passengers, including Matilde and Enricheta, refused to give him anything. He shrugged and took a heaping plate of food up to Manuel in the wheelhouse.

That evening, when I checked into the Galeón Azul hotel, I was feeling a bit queazy. At first I thought it might be from the boat ride. But by the time I'd signed the register and taken my luggage up to my room on the second floor, I began to suspect I was in for a bad night. Which was too bad, because the view of the harbour out my window was spectacular, the hotel itself very pleasant and interesting. Everything was in pale wood and decorated like a ship's interior. People were enjoying drinks outdoors on the terrace, and down in the bar the sweet music of Mercedes Sosa was playing, interspersed with, of all things, songs in English by Alanis Morissette. The smell of food from the restaurant was both enticing and nauseating, and though I would rather have been out exploring, I took a Gravol and lay down in bed. Unfortunately, the Gravol was either too late, or the bug too virulent, because an hour later I was violently ill. As to cause, all I could think of was the oyster chowder served by Cervantes on the *Maritza del Carmen*. I wondered if Matilde and Enricheta, by now on their way home with their father, had been similarly afflicted. Somehow I doubted it. Feeling sorry for myself, I offered up prayers to the painting of a Chilote wooden church above the minibar, and wished Catherine had been there to commiserate. Between bouts of strenuous regurgitation, I lay on my bed, weak and perspiring. When it grew dark out, I crawled between the sheets. Down on the ground floor, Mercedes Sosa and Alanis Morissette were doing their best to console me with lullabies, but even so, it was not a good night. In fact, it was by far the worst night I spent in South America.

In the morning, I scrapped my plans for a leisurely stroll along the boardwalk that fronts the hotel and leads to Fuerte San Antonio. Somebody, either señor Ibañez, or Arturo, the Don Luis desk clerk, had told me I should make every effort to visit the fort, which has a fine museum and where I'd be able to see the rusty cannons left behind in 1826 by the fleeing Spaniards. Sorry, but I was in no mood to look at cannons, rusty or otherwise. Even if they'd brought one to my room and offered to fire it, I'd have said no. At ten o'clock, the heartless chambermaid, ignoring the sign, "No Me Moleste, por favor!" knocked and called out, "Domésticos!" So I dragged myself downstairs and found a table on the patio, but all I managed for breakfast was a cup of tea with lemon in it. Which was probably just as well, as I'd taken no insulin since the previous morning. My appetite was not helped by the fact that the people at the table next to me, three men and a woman, were eating what looked like eels poached in buttermilk.

By two o'clock, I was not only on the road to recovery, but also on the road to Castro, two and half hours away by Cruz del Sur bus. Even had I wanted to stay at the Galeón Azul a second night and try the eels in buttermilk, it would not have been possible, because all sixteen of its rooms were spoken for. The helpful desk clerk, whose name was Gomez, said he thought the nearby Hostería Lluyhay still had space, and was willing to phone, but by then I had my bus ticket and was anxious to be on my way. I'm not sure why.

It's about 150 km from Ancud to Castro. The north-south highway connecting the two towns is called (for reasons which escape me) the Pan-American. Just south of Ancud, at a village called Coquiao, a swarthy, overweight man in blue jeans and fringed leather jacket climbed aboard and sat next to me. He sported a ponytail, but no luggage, other than a yellow canvas handbag which he carried over his shoulder. Our conversation went something like this:

"Buenas tardes, señor."

"Good afternoon."

"Habla usted inglés?"

"No hablo español. I only speak English."

"No comprendo. Hable despacio, por favor."

"I said, I only speak English."

"Sí, I thought so. Well, I only speak English ver' little. Someday I learn better. My name is Sylvestre."

In fact, Sylvestre spoke English quite well. When I asked him where he'd learned it, he said not from television, not from newspapers, but in a bicycle factory. This made no sense, but I didn't pursue it. He said he lived in the town of Mocopulli, which we would come to later in the trip, and that he was an employee of Parque Nacional Chiloé. Reaching into his handbag, he took out two pepper-stuffed empanadas and offered me one. When I shook my head and said, "No, gracias," he proceeded to eat them both and lick his fingers. If his empanadas had been stuffed with eels, I might very well have left the bus.

Not far from Coquiao, Sylvestre pointed at a dirt track branching off the highway and said that prior to the 1960 earthquake, this had been the roadbed of a narrow-gauge

railway running south to his town, Mocopulli. Unfortunately, the damaged railway had been abandoned after the earthquake and never restored. Was this not sad? I told him I
came from Canada, where a single railway stretched across
the entire continent. He was not visibly impressed, nor did
he ask me about polar bears.

A little further on, Sylvestre reached into his canvas
handbag and pulled out a jar of what looked like molasses,
but smelled strongly of pumpkin. He called it *dulce de cal-
abaza* and began eating it with a spoon. He seemed to know
better than to offer me any, although had he, I think I might
have tried it.

One thing about having Sylvestre beside me for most of
the bus trip—his chatter kept my mind off my uneasy gut.
Luckily, he didn't require me to talk, and as long as one did-
n't expect anything intellectual, he was mildly interesting.
Not at all like señor Ibañez, whose English was not as good
and who had seemed intent on instructing. Sylvestre prattled
on about a variety of things. He spoke of a beautiful wooden
church in the southern village of Pindapulli, built by the
Jesuits in 1755. He spoke of his job in the Parque Nacional,
and his task of keeping an eye on the coastal colonies of Magellanic penguins. Every time we passed a house whose walls
and roof were covered entirely with shingles, he drew my
attention to it, said it was typical of Chilote houses, and that
when I arrived in Castro, I would see thousands of them. He
may have meant dozens. The church of the Archbishop of
Chiloé, he said, a close personal friend who lived in Ancud,
was just such a structure. When I asked him what kind of
trees the shingles came from, he said these days, mainly pine
and eucalyptus. But the tragedy of Chilean forests was that
their best tree, the majestic alerce, which some people mistakenly called sequoia, was being ground into wood chips
and exported to Japan for paper. While temporarily good for
the economy, was that not a terrible waste? When I agreed it
was, he seemed mildly offended. Was I aware, he wanted to
know, of an even more serious problem—the hole in the

ozone layer over southern Chile? And if so, did I, as a guilty norteamericano, have a remedy? When I said no, he rummaged in his canvas handbag, but finding nothing more to eat, fastened it up and stared disconsolately out the bus window. Only then did I realize that most of the other passengers, of whom there were perhaps thirty, had been listening to us. When I glanced toward the driver, I met his eyes in the rear view mirror and saw that he was smiling. He either didn't know about the rape of the alerce trees and the hole in the ozone layer, or didn't care.

On the outskirts of the village of Degán, where two passengers departed and a road branched off eastward toward the fishing port of Quemchi, there was not only a shingled house but a hideous, pot-bellied mannequin in the front yard. It wore a grimace and a pointed hat, and at first glance reminded me of the grotesque trolls one sees in Norway, only uglier. Somewhere between a statue and a scarecrow. When I asked Sylvestre what it was, he said it was the likeness of *Trauco*, an evil dwarf who roams the island defiling spinsters and virgins. Surely, he said, we must have such creatures in Canada. How else explain unwed pregnancy to children? He also advised me to keep my eyes open for *Pincoya*, a mythical female water nymph, who often appears nude, or only partially clothed.

At Mocopulli he and a dozen others got off, half of them seemingly headed for the nearby coastal village of Dalcahue. Before hoisting himself out of his seat and shaking my hand in farewell, Sylvestre said that while I was in Castro there were two things I mustn't miss: the purple wooden church, Iglesia de San Francisco, and a shingled, seaside restaurant called Octavio, which was built on stilts and served reasonably good curanto. If I had time left over, I might visit the regional museum on calle San Martín and see a bicycle made of wood. The Chilotes were crazy for things made of wood. Even anchors. But, he said, the moment I was finished with Castro, I should pay a visit to Dalcahue's seafood and artisans' markets, where the best mussels, sweaters and baskets in all of Chiloé could be found.

Then he was gone, and strangely enough, I missed him.

Eight new passengers came aboard, but no one sat next to me, and so all the way to Castro, when I should have been watching the scenery, I dozed.

* * *

Chapter 6.

In Castro, Capital of Chiloé.

Guide books differ as to when Castro was founded. Dates vary all the way from 1567 to 1600. There is fair consistency, though, in the date a road was completed from Ancud to Castro—around 1780—and in the fact that Castro is Chile's third oldest city, after Santiago and La Serena.

In bygone days, one of the things Castro was important for, perched on its hill overlooking Castro Fjord, was the provisioning of whaling fleets headed south. That and selling logs for the manufacture of railroad ties. What's curious is the way guide books seem to suggest you can take a bus from Castro to the mainland. To Puerto Montt, for example, or Chaitén, or Puyuhuapi, where Catherine was holidaying. What they mean is, you can get on a bus, drive to the water's edge, and go aboard a car ferry. Then, after several hours, you drive off the car ferry and continue your journey. But you can't simply drive to the mainland from Castro. You can't fly, either, unless you're a goose or a helicopter.

Late in the afternoon, the bus dropped me off in Castro's main square, the Plaza de Armas, which is quite vast and ringed with shops and restaurants. Across the street stood the purple, twin-towered church Sylvestre had mentioned, Iglesia de San Francisco. Had I been feeling better and not burdened with luggage, I might have crossed the plaza and gone inside. Instead, I decided to wait till later and see it with Catherine. In front of me was an official-looking building with the word *Correos* painted across its window. Assuming this to be the post office, I went in and asked a sultry young woman behind the counter if she knew the whereabouts of the Hotel Unicornio Azul. She laughed aloud at my pronunciation, but pointed vigorously northward, downhill, toward the ocean.

For some reason, she kept saying, "Rosado, rosado!" Deciding this must mean pink, I wondered what it had to do with azure unicorns. I tried to ask her if the Unicornio Azul was within walking distance. She had no idea what I was saying, but answered my question without meaning to, when she pointed outdoors and said, "Parada de taxis. Setecientos pesos."

Not until the taxi pulled up in front of the hotel on avenida Pedro Montt and the driver asked for exactly 700 pesos, did I comprehend what the postmistress had been trying to tell me: the Unicornio Azul, the Blue Unicorn, was in fact painted primrose pink.

I've found that some hotels appeal at first glance, others don't. The Albatross in Ushuaia was one that appealed. I could have stayed there indefinitely. Something about its look and feel—the lobby, the lounge, the windows. Other times, I've been fooled. A hotel that looked good, turned out to be terrible. By the same token, some that looked bad turned out to be perfect. The Unicornio Azul in Castro fell into the latter category.

At first glance, I thought, "This place is the work of an architect on mescaline." Besides its odd pinkish colour, the ascending portions of hotel suggested prefabs dislodged by a landslide, or thrown helter-skelter off a lumber truck. True, there were picture windows and balconies facing the fjord, and I could see people enjoying the breeze as they sipped their evening drinks. But because of the jungly appearance of the hillside, lush with arrayán trees and calafate bushes, the impression I had was of the brightly painted tin houses of La Boca in Buenos Aires. As I stood there, listening to nesting chincols screeching overhead, I was afraid I'd made a huge mistake.

But I hadn't.

At Reception, I discovered a plump, older lady who spoke comprehensible English and punctuated her words with hand gestures. On the lapel of her blouse she wore a gold brooch engraved with the name Susana. Right off the bat, pleasing things caught my eye: hardwood floors, a slowly

The town of Castro on Chiloé Island.

turning ceiling fan, two bright blue wooden unicorns, one on
either side of the foyer.

After a short search, Susana found my reservation and
asked for my credit card. Not VISA, not American Express,
but MasterCard, which I didn't have. Nor did I have much in
the way of traveler's cheques. I had no ATM card either, as I'd
been using my VISA card to draw cash from cajeros
automáticos. The irony was that heretofore, VISA and American Express had been readily accepted, but not MasterCard.
Traveller's cheques were sometimes scoffed at. What people
wanted, especially in shops and markets, was cash. Taxi driv-
ers and boatmen insisted on it.

Susana was only temporarily flummoxed. She frowned,
shook her head, clucked her tongue. A young couple behind
me, obviously honeymooners, were anxious to check in. Sens-
ing their impatience, muttering to herself, Susana demanded
my passport, wrote down my VISA and American Express
numbers, had me sign a chit. Then she gave me the key to my
room. I never did find out how she finagled things, but upon
my return home in October, I found that the Unicornio Azul
charges had been billed to my VISA account.

While my room did not have an ocean view, it did look out over the hotel's gardens, where the raucous chincols were still in full chorus. As Catherine said when she first heard them, they sounded like roosters imitating screech owls. Though quiet during the middle of the night, as evening approached they swarmed the treetops and began gossiping.

That first night, after a hot shower, a nap and a tasty dinner of *cancato*, which turned out to be local salmon stuffed with cheese and tomatoes, I felt reasonably restored. The pisco sour beforehand and the glass of Casablanca during might have helped. Though nobody came and played the piano, I did spend an hour looking at the hotel's display of enlarged black and white photographs, which showed fascinating aspects of Chiloé, especially of Castro harbour, back through the years. One whole wall was devoted to earthquakes. At Reception, Susana had been replaced by a boy hardly past puberty. He was decked out in a starched white shirt with gold cuff links, black trousers and a brocaded vest. He acknowledged me with a smile, looked very sure of himself. I asked him if it was safe to go for a walk after dark, down to the waterfront, or up into town, and he said, "Que sí! Claro! Naturalmente! Why would it not be safe, señor? Castro has no criminals, only a few."

That night, for some reason, I had probably the best sleep since arriving in Chile. With my window open and no street noises, only the bellyaching of the chincols and the distant rumble of fish boat engines, I threw myself into the arms of Morpheus and woke up amazingly refreshed. The wind was calm, the sun shining. There was no rain, no fog. According to the guide book, such days in Castro were rare. And so I took a Bufferin for my slight headache, brushed my teeth, and went in search of breakfast. I was pleased to see Susana back at Reception. "Buenos días, señor!" she said, "Hoy es jueves!"

I decided she had just told me that today was Thursday, or else that my fly was open. Either way, it was kind of her. One doesn't get service like that in North America.

After breakfast I set out downhill on foot and walked along the piers. Castro Fjord was alive with fishing boats, coming and going. There were larger boats too, supply boats, cruise boats, even a small flotilla of tugboats, whose purpose I could not determine. On my left stood a dozen brightly painted *palafitos*—buildings constructed out over the water on spindly poles. I could certainly see why they'd collapse during an earthquake. I wondered why they weren't demolished by storms at high tide. On the shores of Lake Superior, they wouldn't last a season. Maybe the waves simply washed under them. If there had been anyone but small children about, and if I'd been able to speak Spanish, I might have asked someone for an explanation.

At what appeared to be a naval dockyard or Coast Guard station, surrounded by chain-link fence, I turned uphill on avenida Blanco. The street rose sharply toward the centre of town, the gradient so steep that cars were parked with their front wheels angled toward the curb. Though it was early, shops were busy, banks open, people bustling along the narrow, fractured sidewalks. Though I was puffing with exertion, no one else was. I stopped often, pretending to be intrigued by window displays. I thought of little Lucia, of walking with her in the rain at Puerto Aguirre. Which made me think of Catherine and wonder where she was at that moment. Up near Plaza de Armas, a church bell was pealing insistently, its chimes echoing over the town. School children carrying books ran by, not out of breath at all. Shouting, in fact. On the point of collapse, I lurched into a crowded café on calle Serrano, with the word "Cantina" lettered above its door. After bright sunshine, the interior was dark, smoky, noisy. Eventually I found an empty stool at the counter and sat down. A short, hairy waiter, in shirt-sleeves and apron, said, "Hola, señor."

"Café, por favor."

"Un exprés? Café solo? Café con crema? Café con leche?"

"Café con crema, por favor."

"Un grand?"

Hillside houses of Castro, capital of Chiloé.

A palafito, built on pilings, Castro harbour.

"Sí, por favor, un grand."

"Y tapas, señor?"

"Sí, y tapas, por favor. Gracias."

"De nada."

He stood before me, waiting expectantly, but I didn't know what he'd asked. Finally he said, "Qué tapas, señor?"

All I could do was shrug. By now, people around me were listening, watching, smiling.

"Anguilas, señor? Caldillo de congrio?"

Again I shrugged. Held up my hands. A few people chuckled. I was on the point of rising and leaving when the hairy waiter said, "Eels, señor. Soup of the conger eels. Ber' good, ber' tasty. You like to hab these, inglés, norteamericano?"

Which made everyone but me laugh uproariously. I was halfway to my feet when the waiter put his hand gently on my shoulder. "Coffee with cream is coming, señor. Un grand. And I think you like these nice torta with fruits. Seat yourself. I bring you these."

So I did, and he did, and people smiled at me. When they got up to leave, they patted me on the shoulder, just as the hairy waiter had done, and said, "Adiós, inglés!"

The large coffee with cream was hot and strong, the cake indeed tasty. When I was finished and reached into my pocket for a handful of pesos, the hairy waiter showed me his palms, shook his head, refused payment. "Eez firz tine in Castro," he said, and walked away to serve someone else, taking my dirty dishes with him.

I spent almost the entire day exploring Plaza de Armas. The sun continued to shine, pigeons strutted back and forth. At noon, the purple church, Iglesia de San Francisco, clanged its bells. A cracked, tarnished fountain in the middle of the square, representing a boy holding a salmon, suddenly gurgled and began squirting water out of the salmon's mouth. Soon after, a flock of wrens flew down and splashed about with the pigeons. Having consumed two breakfasts, I decided to skip lunch, and found a bench under a tree beside a cannon on the west side of the square. All the other benches were occupied by old men, and it occurred to me that in a European coastal town these codgers would be sipping grappa or slivovitz or schnapps or arak or ouzo at a sidewalk café, talking, arguing, playing cards. But here in Castro they simply sat, faces turned skyward, soaking up sun like indolent tomcats. Some were smoking cigarettes, some pipes. When a gaggle of old women walked by, the old men doffed their caps and patted the benches beside them, but the old women kept on walking. A few dogs and small children walked by too, and mothers pushing strollers.

For some reason, there was a long line-up at the Post Office, with people forced to stand in the street, waiting their turn. At one point, a bent old man using an aluminum cane sat down beside me, but when I asked him in English what the people were lined up for, he only nodded his head and laughed. I noticed he had hearing aids in both ears. I said, "Qué pasa?" and pointed at the Post Office, but that accomplished nothing. "Los locos," he muttered, showing tobacco-stained teeth and tapping his forehead.

Though I'd planned to delay my visit to the purple church until after Catherine arrived, at three o'clock, when the plaza was almost empty, I crossed the street and went in. I'd read somewhere that this odd-coloured church was erected at the turn of the century and was now a national monument. Built of local lumber, its facade and spiky spires are painted two-tone lavender and puce. The structure would seem, at first glance, to have been inspired not by the Jesuits, but by Walt Disney. The more one stands and admires it, the more incongruous it seems. A church, after all, should be austere and dignified, should it not? Iglesia de San Francisco in Castro, with its mauve towers and triple-arched facade, borders on frivolous. You expect to see Hansel and Gretel walk out of it, carrying balloons. In a strange way, I almost wished señor Ibañez had been there to offer comments.

Entering, after being out in the sun, was like walking into a darkened movie theatre. Right away, though, you were

Iglesia de San Francisco in Castro.

aware of tall wooden columns soaring overhead. There wasn't the usual clamminess or smell of damp stone that you get in Old World cathedrals. Instead, there was the faint aroma of wood, of dry dust. Your footsteps echoed pleasantly on the floorboards. As nearly as I could tell, I was the only one there. Which was odd. Usually in churches you see a few old women kneeling or lighting candles. Often a priest and choirboys, or a gaggle of tourists having the statuary explained by a multilingual guide. But there I was, alone in a forest of laminated pillars, eyes slowly growing accustomed to the murk. The same strange feeling I'd had at Puerto Aguirre—that of being detached and hopelessly far from home—crept over me. The thought that I was in far-off South America, in a wooden church on a remote Chilean island, nearly overwhelmed me. It was not a pleasant feeling—too much like stepping through the looking glass and being unable to find your way back, or falling through a black hole into an unfamiliar universe. Foolishly, perhaps, on the verge of panic, I turned and bolted for the exit, which was delineated by daylight. Had anyone been watching, they'd have thought I was being pursued. I burst through the door, half-blinded, and hurried back across the Plaza de Armas. I was chagrined to find two men in business suits sitting on my bench, smoking. How dare they! Turn your back for a minute, and someone steals your bench. Why, with so many empty benches, would they take mine? Maybe because it was under a tree. So I went and sat on a different bench, beside a rusty old cannon, and took a few deep breaths. In my mind's eye I retained the image of a wooden statue inside the church, up near the apse, representing a shadowy figure locked in battle with demons. As I rose to leave, I noticed a grizzled, heavyset old man in a brown hat and sweater sitting in front of a restaurant across the street. He looked very photogenic, and was staring at me, and so I took the liberty of approaching him and asking if I could take his picture. He shrugged, which I assumed meant he either didn't care or didn't understand, and so I snapped him. As I turned to leave, he said, "Gorila." I put out my

"Gorila" in Castro.

hand, thinking he had just introduced himself, but all he did was draw back and look at me in alarm. "Gorila," he said again, almost as a threatening growl, sounding like a bulldog. And so I left.

By the time I got back to the hotel, it was after four o'clock. I was tired and parched. I'd walked a long way, covered most of the town. Although my stomach ailment had cleared up, I had a sore throat and blisters on both heels.

And then as I stepped into the foyer of the Unicornia Azul, there was Catherine, sitting in a chair across the lobby from the front desk. My first thought was that I'd lost a day. I hadn't expected her until the next evening. When she saw me, she waved and stood up and came to greet me. It was like encountering an old friend in an unlikely place. The first thing she said was that she was twenty-four hours early. That while the Puyuhuapi Hotel and Spa had been pleasant enough, very posh, very relaxing, she'd quickly run out of things to do. You could stand only so many mud baths and massages, could drink only so many pisco sours. And since *El Bosque*, the Patagonia Express ferry boat to Quellón, on Chiloé's southern cape, was making an unscheduled crossing today, she'd decided to avail herself of its services. The two-hour bus ride from Quellón to Castro, she said, had been interesting, with brief stops in the villages of Chonchi and Vilopulli. As a matter of fact, she'd decided she might like to do more bus travel in the future. From a bus, she said, you could see the countryside, and the way people lived, their houses, their gardens, their livestock. It was also the best way to see mountains. She didn't mind boats, she said, but had pretty well had her fill of islands, and wouldn't care if Chiloé was her last one.

Her room was on the floor above mine and faced Castro Fjord. After showering and changing clothes, I met her there and we had drinks sent up. We sat on her balcony, under the leafy branches of an arrayán tree, whose foliage was so thick we were bathed in diffuse green light. A warm breeze wafted in off the ocean, carrying sounds of the waterfront, and had it not been for the nattering of the chincols, the setting would have been idyllic. I told Catherine about my visit to the purple church and the momentary feeling of being lost in space. She said the same thing had happened to her one day in Santiago. She said that on the bus from Quellón she'd sat next to a woman from Chaitén, whose parents were both descended from Mapuche Indians. She'd told Catherine that in pre-Columbian times, there had been a million Mapuch-es living in Chile's Austral region. They were a fierce, inde-pendent people, who had resisted everyone from the Incas to the Spaniards. She said that after the introduction of the horse, the Mapuches had ridden up and down the Andean coast, spreading their language, culture and spirituality, teaching other indigenous people how to herd guanacos. But the thing the Mapuches were best known for, she said, and were still very good at, was silver-smithing. Their silver jew-elry was the best in all of South America, if not the world. They also knew a great deal about herbal medicine, and about those ancestral deities who inhabited the snowy peaks of the Andes.

Catherine said that in one sense, it had been a fascinating, educational bus ride, and when the woman, whose name sounded something like Pillanes, had disembarked at Chonchi, she'd been sorry to see her go. She said she'd been hoping for an invitation from señora Pillanes to come and visit her, but no such invitation had been issued. "I'd have suggested it myself," she said, "but you can't force yourself on people. Not in a foreign country. After she got off, it occurred to me that historically, distrust of strangers was probably ingrained in her."

Catherine said she'd had no trouble using her VISA card at Reception when she checked in. As a matter of fact, Susana, the desk clerk, had told her that they preferred VISA to MasterCard. She'd also informed her that another Canadian, a señor MacDonald, was registered at the hotel. "Qué casualidad!" she'd said. What a coincidence.

We took a taxi down to the harbour and had dinner at the restaurant recommended by Sylvestre—Octavio. This turned out to be a crowded, two-storey, shingle-covered edifice built out over the water. The dark pilings it sat on were encrusted with snails and barnacles. On its west wall was a large sign advertising the house specialty—*curantos*, which is a vast melange of fish, clams, oysters, sausages and potatoes, served piping hot in wooden bowls. It took us two hours to get through ours, at a table overlooking Castro Fjord. We were hovered over by an elderly, potbellied waiter named Enrique, who said he could speak English. I'm not saying he couldn't, but he was totally incomprehensible. Not that it mattered. He kept our wine glasses filled, brought us fresh napkins every few minutes, and babbled away at us, just as though we understood him.

The evening was memorable for many reasons. Halfway through the meal, a full moon rose and shone in the restaurant windows. One of the waiters went and turned down the lights, so that the room was illuminated only by the moon and candles. Authentic Chilean music was playing. Over coffee, Catherine said, "I don't mind telling you, I was glad to see you come in the door of that hotel this afternoon. I wasn't sure you'd be there."

"Of course I'd be there. Why wouldn't I be?"

"I wasn't sure just how definite our plans were. When you're travelling, there's always the unexpected. It wouldn't be the first time someone had stood me up."

I was on the point of taking umbrage, but didn't. Lighted ships were passing across the moon's path. A noisy group of people at the next table started singing, and soon everyone, including our waiter, was singing too.

Catherine said, "I'll tell you something else. I don't care if I never see another island. I've about had it with islands. Too confining. Too insular. It's like they have a fence around them, a moat full of crocodiles. I need space. Unlimited space. I'd like to follow your advice and set out for Ushuaia."

"I don't remember recommending Ushuaia."

"No, but you did say it was at the end of the earth."

Enrique brought more coffee, offered us snifters of pisco, which we declined, much to his annoyance.

I said, "So that's where you're going next, Ushuaia?"

"I'm not sure. I mean, I'd like to cross the Andes into Argentina. Visit Bariloche and Calafate. See the Perito Moreno glacier. Set foot on Tierra del Fuego."

"Tierra del Fuego is an island."

"Yes, but it's a *big* island. And you really can't leave South America without seeing Tierra del Fuego. What would Darwin think?"

There was a long silence then. We watched boats pass by in the moonlight, listened to the singing. Once again I had the feeling of being impossibly far from home, but was getting used to it. I was stuffed with *curanto*, mellow on wine. Enrique brought us a new candle, lit it with a flourish.

Catherine rummaged in her bag, extracted a rumpled map of Patagonia, spread it out on the table. Catching me completely off guard, she said, "I don't suppose you'd consider travelling together for a few days?"

At first, I wasn't sure what she meant. "Together?" I said stupidly.

"I think what's missing in my journey thus far is having someone to share the sights with. Not to mention taxis. Someone to help choose an itinerary, get plane tickets. Someone to ride the bus with. I hate to admit it, but I'm finding things a bit onerous by myself, a bit scary. I should have foreseen this before setting out solo, but I didn't. I figured I could handle it. Lots of women do. I've seen them on T.V. Yet at this moment, I'm sorely tempted to pack up and head home. If you hadn't been here in Castro, that's what I'd have done. That was the ultimatum I'd given myself. I'll understand if you say no. Privacy is a precious thing. I probably shouldn't even have suggested it. Blame the wine and the moonlight, and the fact that you're a level-headed person. You seem at ease, very sure of yourself. You also seem to enjoy travelling, as I do. The man I was married to hated it. Wouldn't leave home on a dare. At least, not with me. Of course, there's the other extreme, señor Ibañez. Remember? I'm babbling like an idiot, aren't I?"

Enrique the waiter came over, placed a stubby finger on Catherine's map to show us where Chiloé was, as if we didn't know. Again he offered snifters of pisco, again we turned him down. Though it was late, people were still coming in. Finally Enriche went away with his tray of drinks.

Catherine said, "I don't expect an answer tonight. It was just a passing thought. Probably a stupid one. And I realize you've already been to Bariloche and Ushuaia, so why would you want to go back? I'm clutching at straws, aren't I. It's just that I'm in the market for a knowledgeable tour guide."

It might have been a trick of the candlelight, or the moonlight, or my imagination, but I had the feeling she was afraid of something. It was apparent she wanted to continue her odyssey, but was in the process of losing her nerve. I said, "Did something happen at Puyuhuapi?"

Restaurant Octavio, home of the
best curantos on Chiloé Island.

She looked at me, folded her map, put it carefully away. So help me, her lower lip trembled. For a moment, I thought she was going to cry. But she didn't. She nodded, reached for my hand. I was reminded of holding hands with Maria Malaspina in the lounge of the Hotel Albatross in Ushuaia. She too had been on the verge of tears. What was it in Patagonia that affected women so? Was it too wild and rugged a territory? Surely not. Something in the air, in the water? Ridiculous. I signalled potbellied Enrique for snifters of pisco, chastised him for not bringing them sooner. He looked perplexed, set down two brimming glasses. "Eez ber' nice coctel por lady," he said, giving me a large, ludicrous wink.

I did not ask Catherine what had happened at Puyuhuapi. It was none of my business. To this day, I don't know. But whatever it was had deeply upset her. That was why she'd come to Castro a day early. Sitting there with her at Octavio, sipping pisco in the moonlight, I wondered if the Patagonia Express ferryboat had really just happened to make an unscheduled crossing to Quellón that day. Somehow I doubted it.

"I don't need time to think about it," I said. "I'd be more than happy to escort you to Bariloche and Ushuaia and Calafate and the Perito Moreno glacier. I'd like to see Ushuaia again, and I didn't spend nearly enough time in Bariloche. And I agree, it's nice to share experiences with someone. As I've managed to acquire a modicum of lore from people like Sylvestre and señor Ibañez, I think you'll find my commentary enlightening, if not entirely factual. What I don't know or can't explain, I make up. That's what Bruce Chatwin did, so it's nothing new."

Which made Catherine smile, finally. The moon was out of sight now, having climbed higher than Octavio's shingled eaves. Castro Fjord was empty of boats. Though tables around us were still crowded, the singing had stopped. Our potbellied waiter stood in a corner, yawning. When I signalled him for the check, he blinked himself awake and strode over to us with a large sheet of yellow paper covered in numbers. Though he would have gone through it item by item, in English, I silenced him by placing my VISA card in his hand. He looked at it, started to shake his head, then thought better of it and walked away.

We took a taxi back to the Unicornio Azul and sat on Catherine's balcony in the moonlight. We talked about life in large cities, about people who married for the wrong reasons, about using travel as escape rather than exploration. Catherine said she had an uncle, a retired bank manager, who lived on his investments and travelled twelve months of the year. He'd cruised around the world twice, in opposite directions. He'd been to the Arctic and the Antarctic, spent three months in Australia and New Zealand. He'd taken trains across China, Russia and India. He travelled alone, because nobody could keep up with him. Nobody could stand the pace. He needed to be in constant motion. He had fifty thousand photographs and a million memories, but was neither happy nor satisfied. He was driven by incurable restlessness and hoped to die the day he ran out of destinations. Where he really wanted to go was Jupiter. He was already signed up for Mars. His name, like mine, was William.

Next day, our last in Castro, we visited the purple church, Iglesia de San Francisco. Catherine was impressed, not to say awe-struck. We sat on a bench in the Plaza de Armas and wondered when the rusty cannons had last been fired, and at whom. We walked the length of Encalada Chacabuco and stepped into the Museo Regional de Castro, where we saw a bicycle made of wood. Then we walked back to the Plaza de Armas and had a magnificent seafood lunch at a restaurant called Café del Mirador. In the afternoon we took a taxi west of town to the Museo de Arte Moderno de Chiloé. According to Catherine's guide book, this impressive, wide-windowed museum, set between two hills, "displays the most flamboyant political art in all of Chile." It may very well, but we didn't see it, because the place was closed. The taxi driver, who sat in his cab waiting, had a good chuckle. He could no doubt have told us at the outset that the museum was not open, and thereby saved us the round trip fare. But, as Catherine said, he was a taxi driver, not a tour director. His job was to take people where they wanted to go, not frustrate them with bad news.

Back in Castro, we sat on stools in the smoky cantina on avenida Blanco and ordered coffee from the same hairy waiter who had served me the day before. "Hola, inglés, inglésa!" he said jubilantly. "Bienvenido a Castro. You like to hab some caldillo de congrio? These conger eel soup? These pulpo?"

"No, gracias," I said. "Dos café con crema, por favor."

Serving us, accepting my handful of coins, he said, "So, you like these town, inglés. Now you speak Spanish. Now you hab these nice woman."

At the Unicornio Azul, we told Susana we'd be checking out in the morning and going back to Puerto Montt. She said that rather than go by road all the way to Ancud and take the ferry from there, what we should do, if we wanted to get off the island quickly and cheaply, was let her book us passage on a boat that ran directly from Castro to Puerto Montt every Sunday. The boat, it just so happened, a seaworthy craft, belonged to her sister's husband, señor Paulo. It was called *Monica*, after his daughter. For the trifling sum of twenty thousand pesos, señor Paulo would transport us non-stop to Puerto Montt. With a nice lunch and two bottles of wine thrown in at midday for no extra charge. Plus, if we felt so inclined, any amount of fishing we cared to do en route. Unfortunately, señor Paulo did not accept credit cards, only cash, which was easily obtainable at the casa de cambio down the street, or from a nearby carjero automático. Should she go ahead and arrange the booking?

It seemed like a good idea, and so after the briefest of consultations, we told her to do it. She then agreed to telephone the Don Luis Gran Hotel in Puerto Montt for us and book rooms on our behalf. In this enterprise, however, she was not initially successful: the Don Luis Gran Hotel was sold out for the foreseeable future.

"Did you speak to Arturo?" I asked.

"No," Susana said, "I did not."

"I think you should speak to Arturo, give him our names, promise him a large tip."

So she did, and a few minutes later, with joy in her face, reported that amazingly, Arturo had just received news of a cancellation and could offer us a room after all.

"Solamente *una* habitación," Susana said slyly, holding up her thumb. Not apologetically, but slyly, as though involved in a small conspiracy. "Only *one* room, señor. Puerto Montt eez crowded these week. Eez hosterías completamente fill up."

I looked at Catherine and she looked at me. "We could try another hotel," I said.

"But I like the Don Luis hotel," Catherine said. "And I like Arturo. Ask him how many beds."

"Ah, señorita," Susana said. "I can answer that. All cuartos in hotels of our category hab two beds."

"Then what's the problem? Tell Arturo to expect us."

Which of course Susana had already done.

The last thing I did was ask Susana why the grizzled old man at Plaza de Armas would have referred to himself as a gorilla after letting me photograph him.

"Gorila?" she said. "Gorila eez no eez name. Gorila mean he is bouncer on these door. He hab the box you nose, señor."

* * *

Chapter 7.

From Castro to Puerto Montt;
then to Bariloche, Argentina.

We left Chiloé next morning aboard señor Paulo's blue and white boat, *Monica IV*. Though we ourselves walked down the hill from the hotel to the pier, Susana sent our luggage on ahead in a yellow, horse-drawn cart, driven by her husband and eldest son, Ortiz. Though they insisted there was room for us in the cart too, neither Catherine nor I thought so, and that's why we walked.

The first thing Catherine asked señor Paulo, who looked more Greek than Chilote, with a soup-strainer mustache and bushy black eyebrows, was who the three previous Monicas had been. Unfortunately, señor Paulo had no idea what she was asking, even after several tries, and so she gave up and sat with me behind the wheelhouse, where the sun shone but the wind did not reach.

For the first hour, I thought we were the only passengers. But then at ten o'clock an elderly man in greasy overalls emerged from the forecastle with two steaming mugs of heavily sweetened coffee for us. His hands were black with grime and he had terrible teeth, the same colour as the coffee. He paid little attention to us, stood squinting out to sea as we roared along over the waves. He seemed to be listening to the engine. Just before disappearing below, he turned to us and said loudly, "Maquinista!" We smiled, nodded, thanked him for the coffee. He pointed at his wristwatch, rubbed his stomach, made chewing motions. We mistakenly thought we were having maquinista for lunch. Only later did señor Paulo inform us that aboard *Monica IV* the functions of cook, deckhand and purser were all performed by Bosco, the

Susana's husband and son, Ortiz.

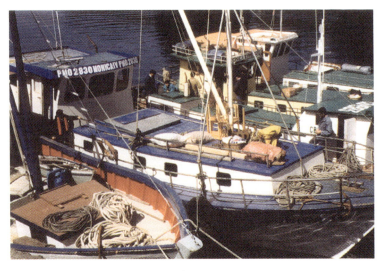

Señor Paulo's Monica IV.

maquinista, or engineer, who was also his father-in-law. This, he said, was both a good thing and a bad. In mainland ports, he could not get drunk and chase women, because Bosco the maquinista would report him. By the same token, Bosco could not do those things either. So it was a trade-off.

Crossing the Gulf of Ancud, I was surprised at the amount of shipping. There were boats of all shapes and sizes, some flying foreign flags. Everything from trawlers to small freighters and container ships. It was exactly like cruising the west coast of Norway from Bergen to Kirkenes. After lunch, señor Paulo drew our attention to the *Skorpios*, cutting a fine wake on a southerly course. He also pointed out a patrol boat of the Chilean navy, which he said was chasing after drug runners. "Everywhere eez drug smuggle," he lamented, rolling his eyes. "Everywhere eez waste my time."

Though I had missed stopping at the fishing village of Calbuco on my outbound voyage aboard *Maritza del Carmen*, we tied up there briefly on the return. I hadn't realized it, but Calbuco, though on an island, is connected to the mainland by a low causeway. We arrived at high tide and had trouble making fast, seemingly because Bosco, the maquinista, señor Paulo's father-in-law, was reluctant to climb down a set of slippery steps. He was quite adamant, and though señor Paulo tried everything, from pleading with him to speaking sharply, the old man stood his ground. "Cobarde!" señor Paulo said, not with real anger, yet half-seriously.

Finally, señor Paulo seized two items that had been lying on deck in plain view, a stuffed magenta garbage bag and a wicker basket. These he threw down to a man on the wharf below. The man made no attempt to catch them or break their fall, only stuck out his foot to keep them from bouncing. Then he picked them both up, threw the bag over one shoulder and hurried off toward a waiting car. It was all very clandestine, very mysterious. Nor was señor Paulo about to offer any explanation. He got back in his pilot house, revved his engine, and pointed the *Monica's* bow toward the shipping channel. Through the window we watched him light a cigar and take a swig from a wine bottle. Catherine and I returned to our roost at the stern, even though Bosco the maquinista tried to inveigle us down into the forecastle by holding up two coffee mugs. "No way," Catherine said. "He'll have to do better than that."

I agreed, because by then we were encountering a westerly chop, which made the *Monica IV* pitch and wallow. It seemed to me the best place to be was on deck.

"What do you think?" Catherine said, "Drugs?"

"Heroin," I said. "Though why he'd be transporting smack from Chiloé to the mainland baffles me."

"No wonder he keeps an eye open for patrol boats."

"I'm just glad there was no shooting."

"The maquinista would have protected us."

"It would've been every man for himself."

"What I'd hate to do is spend the rest of my sabbatical in a Chilean prison, accused of aiding and abetting a drug lord. The trustees on the school board would take a dim view. I can see the headlines."

Which tickled her funny bone, as it did mine, and sent us into gales of laughter. It also made señor Paulo glare out his window at us. At the same time, it convinced me, if I'd needed convincing, that Catherine had the makings of a blithesome traveller.

We spent only two days in Puerto Montt at the Gran Hotel Don Luis, just long enough to have our laundry done and plan a tentative Argentine itinerary. On our first day, at Arturo's urging, we hiked the length of the waterfront boardwalk, the *costanera*, and found ourselves in the portside suburb of Angelmó. We stopped for a seafood lunch at Brisas del Mar, one of the many palafito restaurants on (or rather *in*) the water, overlooking Isla Tengo across the bay. Not only was the entire menu printed on yellow boards outside, but you could buy wine and empanadas to take home with you. When we were leaving, Catherine persuaded our two waitresses, Maria and Rosetta, to pose in the doorway with me and have their picture taken.

Maria and Rosetta at the Brisas del Mar, Puerto Montt.

In the afternoon, when the sun disappeared and a cool, dusty wind sprang up, Catherine bought a beautiful handknit sweater from an *artesania* on avenida Angelmó. We debated stopping at the Juan Pablo museum on avenida Diego Portales (named after Pope John Paul II, who visited in 1988), but in the end didn't, because we were tired, and because the café Xavier, directly across the street, beckoned with a sign promising *cerveza fría*—cold beer. "Refreshment before culture," Catherine said. Words to live by.

We took Arturo's advice and dined in style that night at the Club de Yates (the Yacht Club), which sits on the end of a wharf jutting out into Puerto Montt Bay. As soon as the maître d' realized we were Anglos, he assigned us to a blond young waiter named Steffan, who was Chilean by birth but had lived most of his life in Florida. He had returned to Chile, he said, to visit his maternal grandmother, a German lady living in Puerto Varas. He said he'd forgotten most of the German he'd learned as a child, but not his Spanish, and was

Shopping for sweaters on Avenida Angelmo in Puerto Montt.

practising to become tri-lingual. He assumed that Catherine and I were husband and wife, and commented on our Canadian accents. He knew we were tourists, he said, not because Catherine was wearing her new Chilean sweater, but because we avoided ordering eels off the menu. Locals, he said, always ordered eels off the menu.

Next day, having decided we'd rather fly to Bariloche than take the lengthy and expensive boat and bus trip over the Andes, we went to the municipal tourist office on the costanera to see if this could be done. To our chagrin, they said it couldn't. There was no direct flight. There was no indirect flight, either. Not unless we wished to fly to Santiago, from there to Buenos Aires, and then to Bariloche. Or, in the opposite direction, to Puerto Natales, then Calafate, then Bariloche.

"You must be joking," Catherine said.

They weren't. Instead, they were anxious to sell us bus tickets, boat tickets and hotel tickets for an arduous but scenic two-day journey through the mountains, much like the one I'd made in September. Cash preferred, but credit cards in a pinch. Traveler's cheques only as a last resort, with a processing fee. I wondered if the white cat would at least be there to bid us farewell at the border.

The next thing I knew, Catherine had me by the arm and we were back out in the street. "I must have misunderstood Arturo," she muttered. "I thought he said there were scheduled flights from Puerto Montt to Bariloche on Aero Chaitén."

"Well," I said, "you'd think the tourist bureau would have a better handle on things than a hotel desk clerk. Besides, the overland trip isn't that bad, if you don't mind boats and buses."

"I'd rather fly," Catherine said, and we started back to the hotel to have a little chat with Arturo.

Halfway there, we passed a kiosk with the words "Viajeros/ Travellers" stencilled across its narrow window and a spanking new Union Jack flapping on the roof. It was so small and full of people reading brochures that we barely fit inside. When it was our turn at the wicket, Catherine asked the pert, yet wary-looking young attendant if she knew of any direct flights from Puerto Montt to Bariloche. "Three times a week, luv," the attendant said with a Cockney accent. "There's one tomorrow. Aero Chaitén. Eleven o'clock in the morning. A wee plane, mind you. A puddle-jumper. No lunch, no bathroom. You takes your chances."

Catherine gave me a smug, I-told-you-so look. To the attendant she said, "Do you happen to know where one would inquire about tickets?"

"You'd inquire here, luv. Shall I sign you up?"

"Is there space?"

"There is, luv. It's not what you'd call a popular flight. Not at this time of year. Sort of experimental. Most folks go by the scenic, overland route via Peulla. Takes two days, but no limit on baggage. How many tickets, luv?"

"Two please. One-way."

"How will you pay me, luv?"

"I don't suppose you take credit cards or traveler's cheques?"

"We do, luv. Lloyds Bank. VISA. MasterCard. Cirrus. Thomas Cook. American Express. Could I have your name and address for the computer, luv? And your phone number? And the name of the person accompanying you? Flight leaves at eleven, luv. Boarding starts at ten-thirty. It's a half hour to the airport. I'll send a taxi to your hotel, if you like. Two small bags each, luv. That's the limit. It's a wee plane, you understand."

On our last night in Puerto Montt we retraced our steps westward along the costanera boardwalk and dined in a small, smoky seafood dive called Café Evangelista, which boasts the widest selection of shellfish in all of Chile. This may or may not be true. What the establishment could have used was more customers. Though facing Puerto Montt Bay and Isla Tenglo, it also has a view of Puerto Montt's busy bus terminal. During the course of our unhurried meal, we watched a dozen buses arrive and depart, most headed north toward Santiago on the PanAmerican highway, but some headed south on the new Carretera Austral as well. When we asked our slow-moving waiter, Gregores, whose English was adequate, if not spectacular, where the southbound buses were going, he said to Chaitén, La Junta, Puerto Cisnes, Puerto Aysén, Coyhaique, Puerto Yungay (his hometown), Puerto Natales (via Argentina) and Punta Arenas (via Puerto Natales). Some would not reach their final destination for days. Chile, he said, was an impossibly long, mountainous country, with too many fjords and too many islands. A nation in need of more railroads, more highways, more airplanes. There were enough boats, he said. Too many boats, in fact. Everybody and his dog owned a boat. In southern Chile, there were ten times as many boats as cars. If you wanted to drive from Puerto Montt to Puerto Natales, 1500 kilometres due south, on a nice, paved road, this was impossible. You either had to go through Argentina, land of brigands and sheep herders, or else go aboard a succession of car ferries which ran only certain months of the year. In what other country, he wanted to know, did you have to resort to so many car ferries? (We mentioned British Columbia, but that meant nothing to him.) And did Chilean transport officials not know that rocks from gravel roads broke car windshields and headlamps as fast as they were replaced? It made no sense. None of it made sense. The whole thing was senseless. He was seriously thinking of going to live in Argentina. We asked him if he'd ever been to Buenos Aires, and he said no. To Ushuaia? No. Calafate? No. Laguna San Rafael? No. Río Gallegos? No. Punta Arenas? No. And he likely never would, having heard that it was a bleak, windswept outpost, full of corrugated tin houses and foreign backpackers. Why would anyone go there of their own free will? It was madness. Total madness.

Early next morning, after a breakfast of scrambled eggs in the minuscule Don Luis dining room on the second floor, Catherine and I again said goodbye to Arturo and Bolívar, only this time I think we all knew it was final. We rode to the airport in a taxi driven by a sullen, longhaired youth who said not a word the entire twelve kilometres. At the airport he declined to get out from behind the wheel and drummed his fingers impatiently as we gathered up our luggage.

I was surprised at the number of aircraft parked on the tarmac. There were at least seven. Others were landing or waiting to take off. All small, with one or two engines, but they did seem reassuringly purposeful. The waiting room was crowded. The only place we could find to sit was in a corner beside the lavatory door. Two uniformed ladies behind the counter examined our tickets, said the word Bariloche out loud a few times, seemed satisfied. We showed them our passports, but they took little notice. "Mediodia," one of them said, and pointed at the clock on the wall. We assumed that meant noon. Then her partner stuck out a hand and asked for a thousand pesos. "Mil pesos," she said. "Impuesto. Aeropuerto."

Catherine drew herself up indignantly. "Por qué?"

"Impuesto," both woman said at once. "Aeropuerto."

"Ladronas!" Catherine said disdainfully. I assumed that meant extortionists, and wondered where she'd picked it up. Whatever it meant, it made the two ladies bristle. If we thought we'd pulled a fast one, we were mistaken. As we started to walk away, a third woman, whom we hadn't noticed, came out of an office and pursued us. Apologetically, yet firmly, she told us in flawless English that the two dollars was an airport tax and no one was excused from it. The money, she said, went half to an orphanage and half to the airport for runway lights and new chairs. Did everyone have to pay? Yes, everyone had to pay: no exceptions. Even the locals? Well, no, not the locals. Who, then? Only turistas, señora. That is to say, those who could afford to enter the country and were now leaving it. Was there a similar charge for arrivals? No, señora, only for departures. And it was, after all, only one dollar per person. At Dallas airport, and again in Miami, she herself had been required last year to fork over ten American dollars!

Catherine continued to argue for a while, but then, as an announcement crackled over the loudspeaker and mentioned the word Bariloche, she gave the woman a thousand peso note and they shook hands good naturedly.

The plane we boarded was a twin-engined Beechcraft. Besides the two of us, there were ten other passengers, in single seats on either side of a narrow aisle. The two pilots looked hardly old enough to drive cars, let alone fly airplanes. The younger one made a short speech in Spanish, pointed at the door which had just been closed behind us, handed out small bottles of mineral water. Then he removed his hat and coat, sat down in the right hand seat and put on a headset. A moment later the engines roared into life and we began taxiing away from the terminal. I hadn't seen our luggage, so hoped it was aboard. Catherine sat directly in front of me. Across the aisle from us was a family of four—a mother and three adolescent daughters. The other passengers were all men, some in suits, some in leather jackets. A few had newspapers. I believe one had a laptop. Something in a flat box that he held on his knee and looked at during the entire fifty-five minute flight.

Within seconds after takeoff we were enveloped in cloud. The noise of the engines precluded sleep as well as conversation. When I looked across the aisle at the children, I saw that they all had their hands folded primly in their laps and were staring straight ahead. Their mother, conversely, kept looking out the window, even though there was nothing to see. Ten minutes later, we emerged into bright sunlight above a glittering white layer of cloud. I'd hoped it would be a clear day, so that we could see the lakes and jungle I'd crossed on my way to Puerto Montt, but it was not to be. The ground was invisible. All we could see was the occasional mountaintop poking through. I wished I'd had a map and been able to recognize the volcanoes we flew over. When I judged we were crossing the border, the clouds miraculously disappeared. Now there were lakes, mountains, forests in every direction. Out my window, in the hazy distance, just about the time the engines changed their pitch and we began our descent, I saw the southwestern shore of Lago Nahuel Huapi and realized for the first time just how immense it was. Down below I saw what I took to be Monte Tronador, the region's highest peak. Along its flank you could faintly make out the natural valley running east to west, known as the Paso de los Vuriloches, through which, according to Catherine's guide book, the Mapuche and Chonos Indians traversed the Andes in the old days. Had we been flying over Austria, I suppose it would have been the alpine Brenner Pass. Banking and descending toward the southern extremity of Lake Nahuel Huapi, you could see the many ski hills surrounding Bariloche. Then chairlifts and hilltop chalets came into view. The scene reminded me of hopping the Rockies between Banff and Jasper. It was easy to understand why Bariloche was referred to as the ski capital of South America, and why hordes of Brazilians owned fancy vacation homes here, doubling the local population during snow season. It was also apparent why, if they'd wanted reminders of Bavaria, fugitive Nazi war criminals had sought refuge in Bariloche during and just after the war.

Finally we landed, setting down smoothly but not quietly. The children across the aisle looked visibly relieved, while their mother now began to fidget and make her presence felt. As we disembarked, I saw why. A handsome man in a caramel-coloured suit was there to meet them at the gate, and later I saw them all get into a shiny blue Mercedes and drive away. Catherine saw them too, and as we were going through Argentine customs and immigration (where the officer in his brown uniform gave us a wide smirk when he observed from our passports that we were not husband and wife), she invented the following scenario: the woman had been to Puerto Varas to see her lover and was now home with her husband. She'd taken the children along as camouflage and during the tryst had left them with their grandparents. No wonder she looked nervous deplaning. It would kill her to lose her fine house, her fine car, her fine children, her fine husband. But the truck driver in Puerto Varas was so strong, so handsome. What to do, what to do? We were still pondering this as we retrieved our passports, freshly and officially stamped, and caught the shuttle bus for downtown.

After Castro and Puerto Montt, Bariloche seemed crowded, congested, noisy. Traffic in the streets was heavy. Cars sped by, oblivious to pedestrians. As Catherine said, it wasn't as bad as Santiago, but still took getting used to.

The shuttle bus dropped us off at the Centro Cívico, right in front of the Secretaría Municipal de Turismo. The first thing we noticed, in the middle of the square, was a tall bronze statue of a man on a horse. There was a stiff breeze blowing in off the lake. Teenagers in bluejeans were lounging everywhere, munching apples, guzzling cans of Coke. Inside the Tourist Office, we learned two things: first, the man on the horse was General Julio Roca, who arrived in the mid-1800's and put to flight the resident natives. His noble achievement was called the Conquista del Desierto. And second, the teenagers, according to Esquel, a prissy functionary in leather vest and open-toed sandals, who lisped when he spoke English, were on

General Julio Roca's statue at Bariloche.

Highschool students on spring break at Bariloche.

spring break from their high schools in the nearby towns of Puerto Frías and San Martin de los Andes. Like us, they were turistas. They were waiting, Esquel said, for a City Tour which was due to leave in half an hour, in wagons decorated to look like a train. If we wanted tickets for the tour, he could sell them to us at a reduced rate. We told him that the first thing we needed was a hotel, not a City Tour in wagons decorated to look like a train.

Surprisingly, Esquel turned out to be knowledgeable and efficient. Though he himself would not exchange our Chilean pesos for Argentine pesos, he did send us across the plaza to a casa de cambio that did. The currency he preferred, he said, was crisp new American dollars, which were exactly equivalent to the Argentine peso. But why bother with paper money anyway, when one could just as easily use plastic. After sizing us up and taking note of our simple luggage, he deduced that we wanted something between campground and five-star. I noticed a poster advertising the Hotel Edelweiss on avenida San Martín, which he deemed too costly for what they offered. Did we want private bathroom facilities? Yes. In that case, half the places on his list could be eliminated. Did we wish to stay at a casa de familia? No. In that case, he could quickly narrow it down to three hotels: Hotel Campana, Hotel Internacional and Hostería Posada del Sol. Which did we like the sound of? Catherine said the first one, Hotel Campana. I agreed. Esquel said it would have been his choice too, except that it was situated a long way off, far from any points of interest, with no view of Lago Nahuel Huapi. Not only that, it lacked a restaurant and there were no good ones nearby. Well, then, which would he recommend? Unfortunately, as an impartial civic employee, he was not allowed to make recommendations. Would we care to choose again? Catherine named the second one, Hotel International. Well, fine, but that hotel, while endowed with a restaurant and reasonable prices, was bounded by ugly highrises and not in the best neighbourhood. In fact, it was even further away than Hotel Campana. Whether or not any of these descriptions was accurate (we soon discovered they weren't), there remained only one choice—Hostería Posada del Sol. Were we sure? Yes, quite sure. Good, because he could vouch for it. He knew its owners. By coincidence, they were related to him on his mother's side. Breakfast was included. He would phone and see if they had space available. Two beds or one? Lake view or city view? How many nights? Did we have valid credit cards? Did we require parking? Catherine said she'd prefer a non-smoking room. This made Esquel raise his eyebrows. In his experience, he said, no distinction was made between smoking and non-smoking. That, he said, would be like saying you preferred non-alcoholic beer or decaffeinated coffee or sugarless toothpaste. Someday, he said, such big-city choices might be available in Bariloche, but at the moment, no. Not unless you were willing to shell out two hundred dollars a night at the Edelweiss or Panamericano. Would we, in the meantime, like him to arrange for a taxi to take us to the hotel of our choice, the Hostería Posada del Sol? We asked him if it was too far to walk, and he said yes. So we accepted his offer of a cab. Now, then, what about tickets for the City Tour, which departed from the statue of General Roca every two hours? Maybe tomorrow. Well, fine, but it was wiser, safer, cheaper to buy tickets now. With many students in town for spring break, space could not be guaranteed.

Because he'd been so patient, so kind, so helpful, we bought two tickets for the City Tour.

The taxi ride was barely three blocks long. On the way, we passed the Hotel Internacional, which had no highrises anywhere near it. The Posada del Sol was nice, though, a stone's throw from the lake shore, with views of the Plaza Italia and Puerto San Carlos. Our room was bright and breezy, with a balcony, two beds and three windows. There were no bathrobes or baskets of fruit, no face cloths or bottles of champagne, but there was soap, a telephone, an empty minibar, a colour T.V. with three channels. As Catherine said, what more could anyone want?

After freshening up, we went out in search of lunch. It was a beautiful day to be walking. There were whitecaps on

Lake Nahuel Huapi and a dozen sailboats flitting across the blue water. Though it was too hazy to see distant snowcapped mountains, we knew they were there, because we'd spotted them from the airplane. On the same street our hotel was on, Villegas, we found a packed restaurant called El Boliche de Alberto. We had no idea what boliche meant, although Catherine thought it might have something to do with bowling. On a sign above the door was the word Parrilla, which her small dictionary said meant "Grill." Inside, we found most people eating pizza rather than steak, and no one eating fish. So we ordered a large pepperoni pizza from a waiter in a well-daubed apron. Plus a bottle of Colina de Oro. Then we settled down to enjoy our first meal in Argentina.

Later, we meandered over to the Centro Cívico for a word with Esquel about hotels. But he was gone for the day, replaced by Caleta, a girl in a blue blazer, white skirt and red shoes. Would we care to buy tickets for the City Tour tomorrow, in wagons decorated to look like a train? No, we already had tickets for today. Caleta looked doubtful. "De veras?" she said, shaking her head. Highly improbable. The last tour of the day had just departed with wagons full of high school students from Puerto Frías and San Martin de los Andes. Fine, we'll use our tickets tomorrow. Or the next day. Sadly, señor, señora, today's tickets will not be valid tomorrow. New tickets will be required. That is the regulation. In the meantime, did we need a personal guide, a taxi back to our hotel, access to pizza, movie rentals, mountain bikes, kayaks, tickets to a striptease show? You name it.

"It appears civilization has caught up with us," Catherine said.

Back at the hotel, I took the tattered telephone directory out of the dresser drawer and looked up the name Malaspina. There were seventeen listings, but no Maria. I doubt I'd have called her anyway. Not with Catherine there.

* * *

Chapter 8.

From Bariloche to Trelew & Puerto Madryn

"Puerto Madryn was a town of shabby concrete buildings, tin bungalows, tin warehouses and wind-flattened
gardens. There was a cemetery of black cypresses and
shiny black marble tombstones. The beach was grey
and littered with dead penguins. Halfway along was a
concrete monument in memory of the Welsh. A hundred and fifty-three Welsh colonists landed here off the
brig *Mimosa* in 1865. They were poor people, refugees
from cramped coal-mining valleys and from Parlia-
ment's ban on Welsh in schools. The Argentine government gave them land along the Chubut River."
—Bruce Chatwin: *In Patagonia.*

We stayed three days in Bariloche and the weather was perfect. Bright sun, calm winds, a little afternoon haze. We took
a morning cruise on Lago Nahuel Huapi, which gave us a
good view of the mountain called Cerro Otto, just west of
town. According to the tour guide, señora Belgrano, a dowdy
woman our age who spoke breathlessly into her microphone,
and whose spiels in German and English were nearly indis-
tinguishable, this shapely peak reached an impressive altitude
of 2500 metres. We could actually see its summit reflected in
the lake. Señora Belgrano recommended ascending it by chair
lift after the boat tour, and offered to sell us the necessary bus
tickets to get there. Later, of course, we found that though
you had to pay to go up the mountain, the bus tickets from
our hotel would have been free.

At the summit of Cerro Otto we enjoyed a fantastic view
of lakes, mountains and ski hills. We lunched on roast beef
and red peppers in a revolving restaurant, which wasn't

revolving that day, due to mechanical problems. Only once before in living memory, according to our rail-thin waitress, had this ever happened, and that had been as a precaution during a violent wind storm. Catherine and I imagined the restaurant spinning so fast that dishes flew off the tables and diners tumbled from their chairs. Our waitress had no idea why we were laughing so hard, but said something about wine and altitude.

Coming down the mountain, we negotiated the chair lift without mishap, but then boarded the wrong bus, which dropped us off on avenida los Pioneros in the middle of nowhere. We walked a kilometre or so, saw the correct bus flash by in the opposite direction, finally flagged down a taxi with only one person in it—our waitress. She did not let on she'd ever seen us before.

That evening we went to a movie in Bariloche's only cinema, the Cine Arrayanes, two streets from our hotel. The marquee advertised *Butch Cassidy and the Sundance Kid*, in English, with subtitles. But that's not what we saw. We sat through an hour of something called *Hospedajo Atlantico*, without subtitles, in which laughing young Spaniards danced wildly, shouting and perspiring. Where it was headed was anybody's guess, so we left and went for a walk along crowded avenida Juan Manuel de Rosas. At night, Bariloche, like Buenos Aires, is ablaze with neon lights. Pedestrian and vehicular traffic on the main streets is tumultuous. Our hotel room, with its windows open toward the lake, was a cool, quiet oasis. Since the minibar was empty and I could find no ice on our floor, we sent down for drinks and took them out on the balcony.

Next day we boarded a small red Codao del Sur bus at Centro Cívico and took a tour of the scenic countryside. We visited the very posh resort hotel called Llao Llao (named after a large white fungus and pronounced Yow Yow) where we were permitted to tour the lush, verdant grounds and walk through the hotel's opulent lobby. Catherine said she'd read about this famous establishment, which her guide book referred to as a "national treasure," and seemed to recall that President Carlos Menem had been involved in some sort of scandal while vacationing here. The place looked vaguely familiar to me, until I realized I'd passed it on the boat during the first leg of my journey into Chile. We asked our tour guide, señora Rioja, who was also our bus driver, how much lunch would cost in Llao Llao's sumptuous dining room. She predicted not less than $100 per person, excluding wine. Since you had to be a registered guest, we didn't bother.

In the afternoon, since it was included in the tour, we made yet another ascent by chair lift, this time up Cerro Camapanario, from whose summit we again had breathtaking views. Señora Rioja informed us that what we were looking at down below was mainly Parque Nacional Nahuel Huapi, with its forests and sparkling blue lake. Far off to the west she pointed out the peak of Monte Tronador, the extinct volcano we had seen from the airplane. A Japanese lady in the group asked her why it was called Thunder Mountain, and señora Rioja said that when blocks of ice the size of apartment buildings fell from Tronador's hanging glaciers, the noise was like thunder. On the way back to town, skirting Lago Nahuel Huapi, señora Rioja tantalized us with a fleeting glimpse of Isla Victoria, the lake's longest island, accessible only by boat, in case anyone wanted tickets. Moments later, we pulled up beside a vast field of wild lavender. We were allowed to get out and inhale the heady perfume, but were prohibited from picking a bouquet of flowers. At the time this didn't make sense, but it did later, when we stopped at a rustic church and were besieged by young girls selling bunches of wild lavender.

And finally we stopped at a rural restaurant called Colonia Suiza, which señora Rioja said had been named for Swiss colonists who had settled here long ago. Catherine and I noticed *curanto* on the menu, and ordered it, expecting a medley of seafood. But when it arrived we were dismayed to find it concocted from chicken parts and broccoli. We called the waitress over and tried to tell her she hadn't brought us

Luxury resort, Lloa Lloa (pronounced Yow Yow)
near Bariloche.

The view from the summit of Cerro Campanario
near Bariloche.

what we'd ordered. She looked at our plates, and at the menu, and said, quite theatrically, "*Curanto*, sí, sí, sí!" Everyone was looking at us, so we dug in and found the dish quite tasty. While we were eating, señora Rioja came around to each of us and asked if we'd like tickets for a bus tour next day to Cerro Catedral, twenty-five kilometres to the west, lunch included. I wondered why the name rang a bell, and then remembered that Maria Malaspina's grandfather, Rico Benzacar, had gone to prison in Ushuaia for throwing a political enemy, señor Roque, off the top of Cathedral Mountain. Though Catherine said she'd seen enough mountains for a while, had ridden enough chair lifts, listened to enough tour guides, I talked her into taking this jaunt with me, without telling her why. It felt like something I had to do.

Early next morning we boarded another red Codao del Sur bus and drove south down the side of Lago Gutiérrez. At the base of Cerro Catedral there was a quaint alpine inn, called Hostería del Cerro, and a multiplicity of all-season chair lifts. Our new guide, whose name I didn't catch, said that in winter, during ski season, there were endless line-ups at all of them. Not many norteamericanos came here to ski, she said, because they couldn't tolerate the long line-ups. But, if we were interested, she could register us for one of the many ski schools. Membership entitled you to a discount on lift tickets.

Once again, the view from the mountaintop was worth the cost. Just below the summit we had tea and empanadas in a chalet with picture windows. Sitting there, admiring the scenery, I wondered which of the many precipices Maria's grandfather had chosen for his nefarious little crime. While we were relaxing, our tour guide came over and asked us if we'd like to drive a hundred kilometres further south to the town of El Bolsón, where a commune of Patagonian hippies sold excellent pottery, jewelry and beer. She said that if we were finding Bariloche too crass, too commercial, as many visitors did, then El Bolsón, on the banks of the Río Quemquemtreu, would suit us perfectly.

I could see that Catherine was tempted, but the thought of driving all that way on poor roads, just to see some local handicrafts, did not inspire me at all. Besides, we needed the afternoon for making travel plans. So in the end, we said no. After our tea, we bid farewell to Cathedral Mountain and returned to Bariloche on yet another red Codao del Sur bus.

We both agreed that our next destination should be Puerto Madryn, six hundred kilometres (as the crow flies) to the east, on the Atlantic's Golfo Nuevo. Catherine claimed to have had Welsh ancestors, and while none of them had actually participated in the 19th century exodus to Argentina, she still wanted to see where these brave souls had landed. She said she hoped there had been no Welsh involvement in the slaughter of Indians by General Roca. She didn't think there had been, but wasn't sure. She had a feeling that the desperate immigrants, in search of a new homeland, had been granted territory in northern Patagonia because that's where Argentina's Indian fighters needed a white presence. What she knew for certain was that the early Welsh settlers had suffered horribly in this cold, windy, arid land. Until they got their community established, many had starved or died of exposure. In modern times, of course, thanks to irrigation and hard work, there are farms and sheep estancias. Chubut province, named after the mighty river running through it, is presently one of Argentina's most prosperous agricultural regions.

It was late afternoon by the time we entered the Centro Cívico in downtown Bariloche. Both Esquel and Caleta were there, but Caleta now wore sandals instead of red shoes. When we told them we wanted to go to Puerto Madryn, they said that nothing could be simpler. No fewer than four airlines flew direct flights to the east coast: Austral, Aerolíneas Argentinas, LADE and Kaikén. Not every day, mind you, and not to Puerto Madryn exactly, but to the nearby inland town of Trelew (pronounced Trulayo), which had a bigger airport, longer runways, less fog and less wind. And how would we get to Puerto Madryn from Trelew? By shuttle, señor, señora. By van. By taxi. An hour plus a little bit.

Or, if we preferred, we could catch an overnight bus from Bariloche and drive straight to Puerto Madryn. A long, tiring, twenty-four-hour trip, and not straight, exactly, but east to Ingeniero Jacobacci, south to Paso de Indios, then east again to Las Plumas and Gaiman. That was the route taken by the bus known as El Cóndor. Another bus, El Pingüino, went east to San Antonio Oeste on the Golfo San Matias, then due south through Sierra Grande to Puerto Madryn. If he himself were going by bus, said Esquel (which was very unlikely), he would probably take El Pingüino.

Well, then, what would he recommend? As an impartial municipal employee, he was not allowed to make recommendations. Neither was his colleague, Caleta. It would be unfair to all competitors. What he could do was point out possible pitfalls. So, since the bus ride was strenuous, would there be any pitfalls in flying Austral or Aerolíneas Argentinas? A few, señor. Such as? Such as cost, señor. Fine planes, new planes, probably a Boeing 737, but oh, the price. Well, then, how about LADE. Better, señor, but still pricey, and the land shuttle from Trelew to Puerto Madryn not always guaranteed. Okay, how about Kaikén Lineas Aéreas? Perfect, señor, A brilliant choice. If he or Caleta, his colleague, were flying from Bariloche to Trelew, that is how they would go. By Kaikén Air. Planes not so new, perhaps, not so big, but big enough—the reliable Pilatus. Also, a nice lunch on board. Or if not lunch, then breakfast. And transportation from Trelew to Puerto Madryn included in the fare. Not only that, passengers aboard Kaikén Air were entitled to a small discount at the Hotel Peninsula Valdés in Puerto Madryn. Who could beat that? He just happened to have a supply of vouchers in his desk drawer, sent over by his friend Bernardo, the ticket agent.

So, by the time we left Centro Cívico, we had plane tickets on Kaikén Lineas Aéreas to Trelew, shuttle transfers from Trelew to Puerto Madryn, and a confirmation number for reservations at the Hotel Peninsula Valdés.

On our last evening in Bariloche, we walked back to the smoky pizza restaurant, El Boliche de Alberto. The same waiter, in a clean white apron, gave us a nice booth in a corner under a live, miniature colihue tree. We knew it was a colihue, because when Catherine asked the waiter if it was bamboo, he said no, it was a colihue. From it, he said, flutes and baskets were made. While we munched pizza and drank a litre of Melgari red, two dark-complexioned gaucho cowboys with guitars came by to serenade us. Our waiter went up to one of them, pulled a long reed out from under his poncho, blew a few notes on it. "Colihue!" he said. "For make these Gaucho music."

Later, we took the long way back to the hotel, around the plaza Libertad and along avenida Juan Manuel de Rosas. It was a fine evening, the sky full of fireworks from across the lake, a warm, gentle wind blowing. Traffic was heavy, but cars were moving slowly, their windows open, radios blaring. The streets were full of singing, shouting young people. Catherine said it reminded her of Copenhagen in mid-summer, walking near the Tivoli, except that in Bariloche the youngsters weren't all carrying open beer bottles. As we passed the park beside Centro Cívico, you caught the unmistakable scent of wild lavender. We walked along the lake shore to our hotel, holding hands, drinking it all in. Catherine expressed only one regret—that though we'd purchased tickets the day we arrived, we hadn't taken the City Tour, in wagons decorated to look like a train. We'd kept putting it off, and now it was too late.

We sat out on the balcony for an hour, talking. I learned for the first time that Catherine had two married sisters, one in Ottawa, one in Calgary. She'd also had a baby brother, who died very young. Her father, she said, had been a hard drinker, an unpleasant person. Her mother had finally broken free and made a life for herself. I said that in my case, my father had controlled the family by withholding money and making us beg. When my mother went to work and earned her own money, thereby throwing off the yoke, my father lost his authority and became a sulking ogre. He never forgave my mother for giving me everything I asked for, for undermining his control over me.

Sitting on our balcony at the Hostería Posada del Sol that night, on the eve of our departure for Puerto Madryn, sipping chilled Aljibe and listening to the sounds of the city, Catherine and I concluded that both our families had been a bit dysfunctional, that neither of us had enjoyed a happy childhood. We drank to dysfunctional families and unhappy childhoods. We drank to Esquel and Caleta, to their Centro Cívico, to their hypothetical City Tour, in wagons decorated to look like a train. Down below us, a large yellow cat crouched in the hotel flowerbed, glaring up at us, then wandered off to begin his night's carouse.

Next morning, ten minutes into our three-hour flight aboard Kaikén Air to Trelew, I was wishing we'd taken the bus instead. Though we didn't run into cloud right away, we did run into turbulence. Among the two dozen passengers, there were soon many green faces. Off in the distance, out our starboard windows, we could see a dark wall of nimbus and frequent flashes of lightning. "Zeus throwing thunderbolts," Catherine shouted into my ear. I hoped our pilots were plotting a course around these pyrotechnics, as I doubted our aircraft's capability of flying over them. Whether there was any food on board didn't matter, because it would have been too bumpy to serve it. As we bucked our way across the sky, weaving in and out amongst dark pinnacles and turrets, the crew had all they could contend with, up there in the cockpit. Rain began to pelt the windows and it grew very dark. Now and again we broke into weak sunshine and people would lower their paper sacks, but then have to reach for them again in a hurry as we rose and plummeted. I won't say I was afraid, but had we turned back I wouldn't have objected. The thought of rambling along the highway in a bus, watching sheep on the pampas, was very appealing. Glancing at Catherine in the seat beside me, expecting to find her white-knuckled, I was surprised to see that she was quite relaxed, not at all squeamish, apparently napping.

My particular problem was that I'd expected breakfast. Esquel had said that a meal would be served once we were airborne. On the strength of that, I'd injected my regular dose of insulin before we took off. Now, however, it appeared we weren't going to eat after all. I should have known better. Rule #1 for diabetics—don't shoot insulin unless you're absolutely sure there's food coming. Otherwise you're liable to faint from hypoglycemia, which can be serious.

Fortunately, I had my emergency supply of candy with me. As the first twinges of low blood sugar kicked in, I began popping gumdrops. Catherine opened her eyes, saw what I was doing, said she was glad that neither of us was prone to airsickness.

An hour out of Trelew, the clouds parted, blue sky appeared, all turbulence ceased. We droned on over flat terrain, our propellers glinting in the sun. A young female cabin attendant in a grey tailored suit, with Kaikén Lineas Aéreas badges pinned to her lapel, emerged from the flight deck and passed out meat sandwiches wrapped in paper. Most of them were politely refused. Then she handed out bottled water and tinned beer. She put her hands on her hips in front of a fat man across the aisle from us, who had an unlit cigar in his mouth. Laughing at her, he removed the cigar and showed her he'd already chewed, or eaten, half of it. Looking out our window, Catherine said she saw a winding highway and a solitary bus, heading east. "Probably yesterday's bus from Bariloche."

Moments later, the cabin attendant came by to make sure we all had our seatbelts fastened. She made a diving motion with her hand and shouted something in Spanish. For all I knew, she might have been chastising me for having eaten half of Catherine's sandwich and both cookies.

Descending into Trelew, we could see the Atlantic shore ahead of us. There were farms, too, and sparse herds of sheep.

Except for the proximity of the ocean, I was reminded of northern Saskatchewan. As we descended, I saw that what I'd mistaken earlier for barren ground was in fact short grass. I tried to imagine what it must have been like for the Welsh settlers, arriving at a time when the land was unproductive and uninhabited. As the landing gear thumped down, the flight attendant disappeared into the cockpit, where she apparently felt safe. At least in there she didn't have to look at the pale, moist faces of her passengers.

Glancing out the window, I easily understood why Bariloche, in the Eden-like province of Río Negro, with its lakes, mountains and abundant greenery, was full of people year-round, while here in Chubut province, the real Patagonia, the government had given land away free to anyone crazy enough to take it. Catherine must have been thinking similar thoughts, because as we touched down, she pointed out the window and said, "Tundra."

We stayed in the terminal at Trelew just long enough to collect our luggage, then went out and boarded a green Ford van bearing the sign: Kaikén Lineas Aéreas – Trelew – Puerto Madryn – Sierra Grande. There were six other passengers, five men and an elderly woman. None of them, as far as I could tell, had been on the plane from Bariloche, so I don't know where they came from. They stared at us unabashedly, without suspicion or hostility, but with obvious curiosity. The driver, wearing a faded jeans jacket and orange baseball cap, jumped in the front, greeted us in Spanish, turned on his CD player. Then he started the engine, lit a cigarette, and with one elbow out his window, put the accelerator to the floor.

We ran out of paved road a few kilometres north of Trelew, and for the next hour rattled and banged over hard gravel. The landscape was flat, treeless, featureless. Oncoming traffic enveloped us in thick brown dust and bombarded us with flying pebbles. It was like running a gamut of Gatling guns. With the driver's window open, we were soon all wearing a layer of grit. You could well understand why the windshield was pitted and cracked, why the exterior of the van was so pockmarked. There were no curves in the road, and so our speed was constant—breakneck. The noise was deafening, what with the wind and the roar of the tires, and so it was no use trying to talk. During one fairly smooth stretch, I heard what I thought was snoring, and when I looked closely saw that one of the passengers, a scruffy man in a fleece-lined coat, had his chin on his chest and appeared to be sleeping. He didn't even wake up when rocks the size of golf balls hammered at our fenders and floorboards. When the old woman saw me looking at the sleeper, she shook her head and gave me a large, toothless grin.

We reached Puerto Madryn at three o'clock in the afternoon, having driven the last couple of kilometres on smooth, noiseless pavement. Of course the moment we left gravel, the man in the fleece-lined coat woke up and looked sullen.

I had never been so glad to see fishing boats, waves, open water. The town itself was nothing like I'd imagined from reading Bruce Chatwin. It looked clean, uncrowded. There were trees on well tended boulevards. We saw tin warehouses, but very few tin bungalows. Instead, we saw nicely painted dwellings. We saw a school, churches, travel agencies. On streets leading down to the port on Golfo Nuevo, and on avenida Roca, where our hotel was, we saw shops, museums, restaurants. Because of its lengthy waterfront, the town looked like a smaller, more subdued version of Puerto Montt. There was none of the glitz of Bariloche, none of the noise, none of the frenzy.

The other passengers, including the old woman, all left the van at plaza San Martín, while we stayed aboard and were driven two blocks closer to the ocean. Our hotel, the Península Valdés, on avenida Roca, was the spitting image of the San Luis Gran Hotel in Puerto Montt: Reception on the ground floor, breakfast nook on the second, seaward rooms with balconies. As the van pulled up in front and the driver helped us with our luggage, I reached for my wallet. Seeing me do that, the driver shook his head, showed me a Kaikén

Air manifest with my name and Catherine's on it. "Eez already pay, señor. You no pay." Before I could drag out some Argentine pesos for a tip, he jumped back in his dusty, battle-scarred van and sped away down avenida Roca.

The windows of our room on the third floor looked out over the deep bay known as Golfo Nuevo. Across avenida Roca, which in North America would have been Front Street or Water Street, there stretched a long, natural beach called Playa Tomás Curti. Jutting out from shore were several concrete piers, one of which, to our left, must have been a hundred metres long. Nowhere in Patagonia, except perhaps in Ushuaia, had I seen a longer dock. Moored to it was a flotilla of brightly painted fishing boats.

Curving around to the north of Golfo Nuevo, protecting the harbour from Atlantic storms, bulked the land mass that gave our hotel its name—the Valdés peninsula. These days, the mushroom-shaped, eighty-kilometre-wide isthmus, plus all surrounding waters, is a wildlife sanctuary. At a glance, you could see why the Welshmen came ashore here in 1865, why they chose this landlocked bay as their harbour.

Over the next three days, Catherine and I looked in vain for the Welsh monument mentioned by Bruce Chatwin. Which is not to say it doesn't exist. I'm sure it does. We just didn't find it. Nor did we find any dead penguins. Nor any live ones, either, for that matter. Not at Puerto Madryn. Further south we did, on the beach at the Punta Tombo nature preserve. Hundreds of them, waddling ashore to dig underground burrows and stake out territory, as they do every spring. But not at Puerto Madryn.

We opened our windows to let in the sea breeze, then closed them again because it was too chilly. Not only that, the wind was so strong it made the curtains billow. We unpacked, showered, rejected the idea of a nap, then thought better of it and decided to lie down for an hour. When we woke up, the wind was stronger than ever and it was pouring rain.

As clement as the weather had been at Bariloche, it more than made up for it during our stay in Puerto Madryn. It rained at least a part of every day, fog blew in off the ocean, the wind never stopped. Consequently, we rode city buses, spent time in museums and cafés. We napped, dawdled over meals. Our two favourite restaurants, both within walking distance, both on avenida Roca, were the Cantina El Náutico, for seafood, and Restuarant Pequeño, for spaghetti. Between meals, we snacked on the tastiest empanadas in all of Patagonia, at Empanadas del Bicurú, two blocks from our hotel.

We spent an entire morning at the Museo Oceanográfico, just around the corner, looking at displays of Patagonian sea creatures and land animals. We saw a reconstructed whale skeleton, dinosaur bones, stuffed skuas and petrels. We had tea upstairs in the loft, which also houses a library. That afternoon, in persistent drizzle and stiff breeze, we took an Astro bus tour out onto the peninsula, which abounds in salt flats and lighthouses. On its beaches, according to our guide, whose name was Nonna, you can always spot sea lions, elephant seals, penguins, flamingos. And, if you're lucky, just offshore, the magnificent southern right whale, *Eubalena australis*, who swims ponderously by, showing you the flukes of his tail as he stands on his head. This was the correct time of year for all these, she said, holding out her hand for donations to the Reserva Faunística Punta Loma.

That day, perhaps because of the weather, which was untypically terrible, the animals were all absent. Or, said Nonna, maybe they were there, but invisible in the fog. Normally, there was no rain, no wind. The thing for us to do, obviously, was come back on a nicer day.

On our return journey, we stopped at fogbound Punta Norte and fogbound Punta Delgada, drove through the spooky little fogbound village of Puerto Pirámides. Then we skirted the fogbound shores of Golfo San José. Pointing her binoculars at a small island, which she called Isla de los Pájaros (Island of the Birds), Nonna let out a startled cry and said she'd just glimpsed a large sea lion, probably the biggest she'd ever seen, hauling himself down the beach and into the water. Unfortunately, he was gone now, probably off in search of a penguin for lunch. But we could still count him as a sighting. Gazing seaward, she then said she thought she'd glimpsed a killer whale close to shore, hunting baby seals. Which was not surprising, she said, as a small pod of these bloodthirsty Orcas lives semi-permanently in Golfo San José.

For Nonna, it had been a fairly good day. For the rest of us, somewhat less than perfect. It wasn't a complete bust, though, because just as the tour was ending, what should we see but two adult rheas, those scrawny, flightless birds that look like undernourished ostriches, walking stiffly beside the road. Nonna enthused over them, whispered that they probably had a nest nearby. She vowed she'd never seen them so close to the bus. Weren't we lucky to have come along just when we did. Wasn't she clever to have saved the best for last. Would anyone else like to contribute a few pesos to the Faunística Punta Loma fund?

Back at the hotel, Catherine and I fortified ourselves with tea and Bodega brandy in the lounge, put on sweaters and jackets, and hiked north on the pedestrian walkway that parallels the beach. The wind was fierce, the air full of blowing sand. But only scattered raindrops fell, and we drew strength from the surging waves. There were numbers of crested ducks bobbing in the surf, pretending to be penguins. And gulls, of course. Even a cormorant or two. We walked holding hands and Catherine sang a song about white horses galloping on the bounding main. We went as far as the long pier we'd seen from our hotel room, which bore a sign: MUELLE PIEDRABUENA. We'd forgotten the dictionary, so had no idea what it meant. Catherine thought the first word looked like the British word *mole*, which has to do with docks and breakwaters. The suffix *buena*, she translated as "good." Which left only *piedra*, in the middle. I was bereft of ideas, but Catherine deduced that this looked suspiciously like the

French word for stone, *pierre*. "It's quite obvious," she said. "*Muelle Piedrabuena* means Fine Stone Pier!"

We might have walked out on the fine stone pier, with all its fishing boats roped alongside, but gusts of wind were threatening to blow us off our feet and it had started to rain again. Besides, for all we knew, the sign might have said, "Keep Off Or Risk Being Mauled by Elephant Seals."

Back at the hotel, we took hot showers, put on dry clothes, spent an hour talking to Jorge, the concierge, who moonlighted as bartender. He recommended a day trip south to the Punta Tombo provincial reserve. There, he said, in any weather, the beaches would be swarming with sea lions and Magellanic penguins. Inland, there would be guanacos. If we wished to photograph penguins, sea lions and guanacos, and possibly elephant seals, then Punta Tombo was where we should go. This early in October, mind you, the big bull elephant seals might still be on the beaches of the Valdés peninsula, eating squid and fighting. Not such a bad life, really. Could he sell us tickets for such a tour?

That evening, after a five-course dinner at the steamy Cantina El Náutico, we took a taxi to the Teatro del Muelle (which probably gets its name from the nearby Muelle Piedrabuena) and listened to an amateur song and dance group. At least we assumed they were amateurs. They played guitars and accordions loudly, and got laughs, intentionally or not, from the audience. At intermission, pizza was served on paper plates. Unfortunately we'd just eaten. When we stepped out for a breath of air, the taxi that had brought us was still in the parking lot, so we hired it and went back to the hotel.

The winds had diminished, the rain had stopped, so we went out on the balcony. Across avenida Roca, up and down the sidewalks of playa Tomás Curti, youngsters were skateboarding and riding foot-propelled go-carts. In the latter, four people on two seats, one behind the other, pedalled furiously and attained surprising speed. Steering was iffy, though, and there were frequent crashes, into trees, shrubs and each other. Adolescent shouts and screams assailed our ears. That

At Teatro del Muelle, Puerto Madryn.

children should be outdoors so late at night, expending so much energy, amazed us. When they saw us on our balcony they began hooting and making gestures, and so we retreated and drew the curtains.

At breakfast next morning, and on the Astro Turismo bus heading south to Punta Tombo, Catherine told me about a nightmare she'd had during the night. "I know we made a pact not to discuss former spouses," she said. "But does that include dreams?"

After some discussion, we agreed that dreams fell outside the parameters of our agreement.

In this one, her ex-husband, whose name she revealed for the first time was Timothy, had run off with an Indian woman. Not a native Canadian, but a lady from India. It wasn't the first time he'd strayed. While they were married, he was in the habit of coming in from work, or from Kiwanis, with lipstick all over his face and his clothes askew. He also liked to chauffeur members of Catherine's bridge club home across town after an evening of cards, and would return from these forays in a similar condition. Once, he'd arrived with a scratch on his cheek, another time with his spectacles broken.

Mostly, though, he just returned with lipstick on his face and his clothes askew. The only time he didn't was when she herself went along for the ride. She said that if they'd ever had children, he would likely have insisted on driving the babysitter home, and would eventually have ended up in jail.

"This was all in your dream?" I asked, as our bus bypassed the towns of Trelew and Rowson.

"Of course not," Catherine said. "I'm giving you background information. Setting things up."

Her narrative was interrupted then, because our Astro Turismo guide, a young man this time, Emiliano, whose family owned a large sheep estancia at Colonia Sarmiento, picked up his microphone and informed us that thirty years ago some political prisoners had broken out of jail at Trelew, and after terrorizing the town had been hunted down by soldiers and butchered. Back then, he said, making it sound like the dark ages, Chubut Province had been a hornet's nest. Especially Trelew, which in 1970 had possessed both an airport and a railway station. Now, he said, things were quiet and there was little danger from political activists. The same could not be said for aggressive sea lions, which we would soon encounter on the beach at Punta Tombo.

Catherine admitted she'd never met the Indian woman with whom Timothy had absconded in her dream, but believed her to be a medical doctor. There had been a nasty confrontation, during which Timothy had said some terrible things. First, he said he was leaving because, married to her, he felt worthless. It was time to go and make a name for himself. Then he threatened to murder any children they might have together, or that she might have on her own. "You're insane, Timothy!" she had shouted, waking herself up.

I agreed it was a strange dream, a disturbing dream, but in the end, only a dream. I'd had worse ones.

"I'm surprised you didn't hear me shouting."

"Now that you mention it, I did hear something. But I thought it was probably those kids across the street."

"No, it was me, telling Timothy he was crazy."

"Sounds like you had reason to."

"That's what so upset me. That's why I'm telling you this."

I would have asked for clarification, but just then our bus turned off the road and entered a parking lot. There was another Astro bus already there, plus two or three cars. It occurred to me that in many parts of the world, the place would have been bumper to bumper. There were steep, grassy knolls to the left of us, running down to the sea, and broad sand beaches in both directions. Clouds were thickening overhead, waves washing the shore, but the only precipitation was a velvet soft drizzle.

The first thing Emiliano did, once he had us in a circle around him, was apologize for the apparent scarcity of sea lions on the beach. From where we stood, we could see a total of three. They were spaced fifty feet apart, perfectly motionless, three large logs, three dark blobs of flotsam, evidently asleep. Normally, said Emiliano, there would be many more. Sometimes a bull elephant seal or two. Today, they must all be out feeding. But, he added, when we got close to them, we might indeed find that these three were females with babies tucked in against them. If this were the case, we must be wary and vigilant, because mothers with suckling calves could be expected to attack. Be ready, he said, to run if he gave the signal.

As it turned out, one of the sleeping sea lions did indeed have a calf lying at her side. The other two were alone. None of them did much more than open an eye and emit a series of belchy grunts. The baby swivelled its neckless head and gave us a baleful, bloodshot stare, then went back to its lunch. The furthest sea lion, lost in dreams, flicked a flipper-full of sand over itself. Even at a distance, though, you could smell these massive creatures, and it was not pleasant. Like rotten fish in a barnyard. Emiliano pointed out that not all the aroma was coming from the sea lions: further down the beach was the decaying carcass of an elephant seal, being feasted upon by screeching gulls and skuas. Until he set us straight, we'd thought the birds were fighting over territorial rights to a large, dark boulder.

The dozen or so people in our party, comically cautious, snapped at least a hundred photos of the sea lions. It seemed to me that except for the smell, you could safely have gone and sat on any of them and had your picture taken. Not that I would have volunteered to do it.

While Emiliano answered questions in Spanish, Catherine and I walked a little way along the beach, looking at kelp and seashells and bits of driftwood. It was pleasant, but not spectacular. Compared to polar bears and walruses in the Canadian arctic, three and a half somnolent sea lions on a pebbly Patagonian beach at low tide, while interesting, was not earth-shattering. Perhaps if they'd been fighting. Or mating. Or doing tricks. Anything. I wasn't surprised when Catherine said, "I don't know about you, but after today, I think I might be in the mood for some ice and snow again. How would you feel about setting out soon for Calafate and the Perito Moreno glacier?"

"Before or after the penguins?"

"After, of course! I've paid to see penguins, and I intend to."

Just at that moment, Emiliano pointed out to sea, where the hump, then the flukes of a large whale were momentarily visible among the swells. The animal seemed to be by itself, and did not reappear. Moments later, one of the small children in the party bent over and vomited up her breakfast. Blaming the stench of the closest sea lion, her chivalrous brother picked up a stone and hurled it with all his might, hitting the blubbery creature on the back. It was quite a good throw, actually. The sea lion twitched, bellowed, shuffled about inside its skin. As a discretionary move, we all went scampering along the beach, led by the two shrieking children and their scolding parents. Emiliano, not pleased, brought up the rear. I felt like saying, "But you're the one who warned us to be on our toes."

Magellanic penguins at Punta Tombo.

If sightings of sea lions and elephant seals had been scarce that morning, there was no shortage of black and white Magellanic penguins. We drove a very short distance in the bus, maybe a kilometre, to a flat stretch of shoreline covered with rocks and bushes. We parked in a maze of wire fences, and even before getting off the bus could see penguins everywhere. There were several long columns of them coming up from the surf, heading for a range of grassy hillocks off to our right. They weren't hurrying (afoot, I doubt penguins are capable of haste) but they were purposeful. They stayed pretty much in line, three or four abreast, although there were a few stragglers and independents. Only when you looked seaward did you realize how plentiful they were. The beach swarmed with them and there were hundreds, perhaps thousands, already among the hillocks. Some were sitting, some standing, some digging in the gravel with their beaks. As we walked along paths inside the fence, you could see beady-eyed penguin faces peering out of burrows among the tussocks. They made a curious clucking, rattling sound if you approached too close, but otherwise ignored you. They didn't ignore each other, though. They skirmished frequently, beating their stubby wings and slashing with their beaks, stirring up clouds of brown dust, with which they were pretty well covered. As we soon became aware, and as Emiliano pointed out, quarreling wasn't the only activity they were engaged in—there was also a good deal of vigorous billing and cooing.

I think what disappointed me was that I'd always associated penguins with ice and snow. To my mind, their natural habitat was the frozen coast of Antarctica. I'd been spoiled by pictures of the stately emperor penguin, wearing his tuxedo, looking regal. Here at Punta Tombo, on this gravelly, rock-strewn hillside, digging in the dirt and covered with dust, the small, bad-tempered Magellanics seemed misplaced. As Catherine said—Patagonia was full of surprises. For me, this surprise bordered on letdown.

During our drive back to Puerto Madryn, the sun came out. Emiliano kept up a steady patter into his microphone, telling us that the Magellanic penguin was named after the Portuguese navigator, Magellan, who visited Punta Tombo during his circumnavigation of the globe in the late fifteenth century. Scientists estimate present numbers at around a million. Emiliano went into gory detail about penguins being eaten alive by sea lions, elephant seals and killer whales, and their eggs being enjoyed by gulls, skuas and humans. He gave his spiel in English first, which I thought strange, then in Spanish, and just as he was finishing, the little girl who had barfed on the beach burst into tears. I half expected her brother to pitch a rock at Emiliano.

When we got back to our hotel, the sun was out, the wind had died to a zephyr. It was a beautiful late spring afternoon. Jorge, the concierge, informed us that a large party of Japanese guests returning from the Astro bus tour of the Valdés peninsula with Nonna had reported seeing vast numbers of sea lions, elephant seals and whales. Because there was no fog, they'd actually gone out whale watching on Golfo San José and had seen several mothers with babies. As though that

weren't enough, they'd even seen a bunch of Magellanic penguins. The only thing they didn't see was rheas. After the tour,
Nonna had told them she'd never in her life encountered so
many species in a single morning. It was a day for the record
books. Jorge said he could well believe the claim, because the
Japanese tourists had taken so many pictures they were all out
of film. They had asked him where they could buy more.

* * *

Chapter 9.

From Trelew to Calafate &
the Perito Moreno Glacier.

It's a long way south from Puerto Madryn to the Perito Moreno glacier, jewel of the Parque Nacional Los Glaciares. Just under 1200 kilometres, as the crow flies. A dusty, daunting, jarring bus ride over fearsome Patagonian steppes, across rivers, around lakes and mountains. I assume. I'm not even sure it can be done. In any case, we didn't do it.

When we consulted with Jorge, the concierge at Hotel Peninsula Valdés, who had never been south of Trelew, he said he knew of no direct bus to Calafate. El Pingüino or El Cóndor (he wasn't sure which) followed the coast highway down to Río Gallegos, taking several days and nights to get there, but that would still leave us three hundred kilometres short of our destination. Better, he said, since there were no trains, to fly from Trelew to Río Gallegos on LADE or Kaikén airlines and connect with a bus to Calafate. Or, he said, what he would do, if he could afford it, was fly north to Buenos Aires and start from there. It was always easier starting from Buenos Aires. You could fly directly from Buenos Aires to almost anywhere in the world—Miami, Madrid, London, Lisbon, Paris.

Having decided against El Pingüino and El Cóndor, we asked Jorge to phone Kaikén Air in Trelew and see if he could book us on a flight to Río Gallegos. And arrange land transportation to Calafate. And, if possible, get us a hotel room. All of which Jorge did, and said there would be no problem with any of it, so long as were prepared to leave early next morning. If we were, and had a valid credit card, Air Kaikén would send a van for us at five a.m. The flight left Trelew's Aeropuerto Almirante Zar at seven-forty-five and arrived in

Río Gallegos shortly after noon. From Río Gallegos, we would board an express bus to El Calafate. Barring unforeseen delays, we would reach El Calafate in time for a late dinner at the Hotel Los Alamos.

We told Jorge he was a genius. He humbly agreed, saying that as soon as he became more proficient on computers, he planned to go into business as a travel agent "But you're already a travel agent," we told him, and gave him a huge tip.

We left Trelew's aeropuerto internacional at eight-fifteen in a noisy, rattling, four-engined, propeller-driven Pilatus aircraft, the first I'd ever seen. There were fifty other passengers, most of whom, we learned, were bound for an oil rig somewhere near Río Gallegos. There were also a few men in suits and three or four women.

It was not, as we had been led to believe, a non-stop flight. On our way down the coast we landed at Puerto San Julián and Puerto Santa Cruz, before setting down finally at Río Gallegos. We didn't waste time at either of these airports, staying just long enough to let people on and off and allow the pilot, a squat, affable man with a creased face and flowing mustache to greet each new passenger at the door. His name was capitán Colombres and once airborne, he left the flying to his co-pilot. He came down the aisle, helping the pretty young stewardess serve drinks, talking to people. On occasion, when the sound of an engine changed pitch, he would saunter up to the flight deck, have a word with the co-pilot, then resume his visitations. When he came to us he switched into English, said he'd been to Toronto a number of times. When we told him we were bound for Calafate and the Perito Moreno glacier, he took out a business card, wrote the words "Los Notros – Felipe – Amigos Canadienses" on the back of it, and handed it to Catherine. "In these Parque Los Glaciares," he said, "my friend Felipe hab the albergue, the casito, the hotel. Los Notros. Berry nice. You tell Felipe I send you, he gib you these berry nice glaciar room. Felipe my frien' from fuerzas aéreas!"

We were unsure exactly what he'd said, but we shook his hand and thanked him. Catherine put his calling card in her purse. Just then one of the engines changed pitch and we bounced a bit, so capitán Colombres went back to the cockpit for a chat with his first officer. The next time he came down the aisle, he coaxed a small boy out of his seat, led him up to the flightdeck, held him on his knee. He pointed at all the dials and switches, let the youngster put his hands on the yoke, but curbed him when he reached for the throttles.

After circling out over the ocean to make our approach, we landed at Río Gallegos in bright afternoon sunshine and brisk winds. Inside the busy terminal building, waiting for our luggage, we inspected the shops and travel agencies. At the tourist information centre, under a red neon sign saying EL PINGÜINO, I asked the clerk if there was anything to do in Calafate, besides go and see glaciers. In perfect English she in turn asked how she, a resident of Río Gallegos, was supposed to know what there was to do in Calafate, three hundred kilometres away. Had she ever been there? Once, as a child. Was there anything to do, anything worth seeing? Not that she remembered. People only stopped there on their way to the glaciers. Had she ever heard of something called "Los Notros?" Yes, she had. Notro was a flowering shrub with big purple seed pods. It was also the name of a fine, expensive hotel, eighty kilometres west of El Calafate, directly across the Canal de los Témpanos from the snout of the Glaciar Perito Moreno. It was, by all accounts, the best hotel in the Parque Nacional Los Glaciares, with its splendid views of mountains, glaciers and the turquoise waters of the Canal de los Témpanos. It was owned and operated by a retired officer of the Argentine air force, a certain señor Felipe, who, it was rumoured, had political connections. But, she said, laughing in our faces, there was no hope of getting a room there, because Los Notros, as everyone knew, was booked solidly for months in advance. A person would be better off spending time in Río Gallegos, visiting the museum, the oil refinery,

Information centre at Río Gallegos.

the railway of coal trains from El Turbio. Oh, and of course the lovely rookery of Megallanic penguins, the best place in all of Patagonia to see these flightless birds.

On our way out to catch the Calafate bus, Catherine drew my attention to a large bronze wall plaque chronicling the exploits of Antoine de Saint-Exupéry, the French flyer who opened up the first Patagonian airmail routes in 1929. His novel, *Vol de Nuit*, was supposedly set in Río Gallegos. He referred to it as "the town where the wind blows stones around like feathers." He claimed that on some days, even at full throttle, his plane flew backwards, while on others it was blown off the runway before he could get his engine started.

It was a long, uneventful bus ride. We talked, dozed, watched the unchanging scenery roll by. Our route was perpetually northwest. We stopped only three times: at the dusty villages of Esperanza, El Cerrito and Río Bote. On the outskirts of El Cerrito we crested a hill and looked down into an enormous valley, stretching from horizon to horizon, bounded on two sides by jagged purple foothills that were not quite mountains. There were sheep scattered across the barren landscape, with here and there a shepherd's hovel made of stones. From a hilltop outside Río Bote we caught our first glimpse of shimmering Lago Argentino, the largest lake in southern Patagonia. Not far beyond, a range of blue mountains, running north and south along the Chilean border, reminded me of the Rockies just west of Calgary. On her map, Catherine identified the snowcapped peak of Cerro Bolados, whose yearly ice load contributes to the Perito Moreno glacier.

At dusk we turned off the main highway and headed west toward El Calafate. After consulting her guidebook, Catherine informed me that the yellow flowers we were seeing beside the road were in fact calafate bushes, and that their mauve berries were good to eat. If they were so good to eat, I wondered why we didn't see any birds or animals chowing down on them. Catherine's answer was that the berries, though pretty to look at, needed another month to ripen.

Our room at Calafate's Los Alamos hotel looked out over lush gardens, in which both the bright red notros and the yellow calafate bushes grew in profusion. There was also an aromatic flowering shrub we had never seen before, with trumpet-shaped yellow blooms and spiny leaves. We learned later from Domuyo, the desk clerk, that it was called *taique*.

After checking us in, looking down his nose ever so slightly as he gave us chits for breakfast, handsome Domuyo, oozing charm, was good enough to telephone the Hotel Los Notros for us. After several minutes (the phone lines into Parque Nacional Los Glaciares were notoriously slow), he reported sadly that Los Notros, and all other lodges near the Perito Moreno Glacier, were completely sold out for the next month. While Reservations was still on the line, we showed Domuyo the business card Captain Colombres had given us on the plane. Domuyo read it aloud over the phone, emphasized señor Felipe's name, referred to us as the "Amigos Cana-

dienses" of Capitán Colombres. He put his hand over the
receiver, shook his head pessimistically, pretended to look
concerned. But then suddenly his face brightened, and he
said, "The son of señor Felipe tell me they are book up soli-
do for next day, but maybe these room for you close by solamente Thursday, Friday, no in made lodge. This eez bess he
can do, even for amigos of estimo Capitán Colombres. These
prize eez two hund' fitty-fi dollar."

"Tell them we'll take it," Catherine said.

Although anxious to get to Los Notros and view the glaciers,
we put our time in Calafate to good use. Next morning, at
Domuyo's suggestion, we boarded an Almafuerte tour bus
with thirty people from Chaltén and spent the day at Estancia
El Galpón, a working sheep ranch on the grassy shores of
Lago Argentino. El Galpón's manager and part-owner was a
personable young man named Leandro, who rode up to greet
us on his jet black polo pony, Libertador. Leandro spoke flu-
ent English, having spent his childhood in Texas and Califor-
nia, where his father and uncle trained polo ponies for the
Spegazzini stables. When he realized that Catherine and I
were the only non-Spaniards on the tour, he took us under his
wing. He said he was gratified to see that North American
tourists, other than people like Ted Turner, were beginning to
discover Patagonia.

We started our estancia tour with a stirrup cup in the visitors' centre, then went out in the fields and watched clever
dogs herd sheep. Leandro informed us that there were over
seven million sheep in Santa Cruz province alone. Along with
oil, ornithology and tourism, sheep were the backbone of the
economy. Next, we had a second stirrup cup and went into a
cavernous barn to watch sheep being shorn. Here Leandro
said that while competing countries such as Scotland were
suffering from low wool and mutton prices, Argentina was
not. Their markets were expanding, thank God. The only fly
in the ointment was the recent trend toward farming rheas
and guanacos, which were said to be less destructive to the

environment than sheep and almost as profitable. A perennial problem, of course, especially in hilly country, was the presence of pumas, who, as everyone knew, preferred lambs to young guanacos. The sheep ranchers of Santa Cruz province advocated increasing the bounty on pumas.

After stopping for a third stirrup cup, Leandro took us on a tour of the stables, then led us down to the grassy shore of Lago Argentino, where we saw large numbers of ducks and black necked swans. The latter paddled by unperturbed, looking very stately, very regal, some with chicks riding on their backs. There were also dozens of what looked to me like kingfishers, and several flocks of plovers, which Leandro referred to as *chorlos*.

After our nature hike, it was time for yet another stirrup cup, followed by a lengthy, noisy *asado*—a lunch of grilled lamb and beef, served on long tables and accompanied by piquant sauces and numerous bottles of Sarmiento. I have never in my life eaten so much meat at one sitting, or drunk so much wine for lunch. Halfway through, I went into the lavatory and injected an extra 30 units of insulin. Though I was stuffed, the others at the table mocked my minute capacity.

After that, while I would have preferred a nap, we were given two options: either go horseback riding across the pampas with Leandro, or watch a videotape of Santa Cruz province in the estancia's screening room. Since there was a limited number of saddle ponies available, Catherine and I opted for the film, during which, I'm ashamed to say, we both nodded off.

When Leandro and his equestrians got back, we partook of a final stirrup cup, during which the El Galpón staff put on a stage show of *gaucho* singing and dancing. Then our Almafuerte bus arrived to pick us up and take us back to Calafate. With bulging bellies and spinning heads we lurched aboard, and were escorted for a kilometre or two by Leandro on his tireless, galloping steed, Libertador. Back at the Hotel Los Alamos, trying not to stagger, Catherine and I snuck by Domuyo at the front desk and went directly to our room, where we collapsed, fully clothed, in a gastronomic stupor. I dreamt of being conscripted by the cavalry and galloping off into the Patagonian sunset with a knapsack full of barbecued steaks.

Next morning, at Domuyo's urging, we signed up for a bus and boat tour to the famed Upsala Glacier at the northwestern end of Lago Argentino. We had hesitated, not only because we were still recovering from our trip to the estancia El Galpón, but because the Upsala expedition, with Zaahj Tours, was shockingly expensive. Had it not been for Domuyo's insistence, I doubt we'd have gone, especially as we'd be seeing our fill of glaciers at Los Notros twenty-four hours hence. But Domuyo was very persuasive. He may have got a commission.

The bus was crowded with Japanese couples on a package tour from Lima, Peru. There was also a pair of gay Frenchmen, Guy and Benoit, who sat together in the seat across the aisle from us and held hands. For some reason, perhaps because they heard us speaking English and saw us as allies against the Peruvians, Guy and Benoit went out of their way to be friendly. They spoke to us in their best English, told us they were from La Rochelle, expressed surprise at finding anyone as far from home as they were. Guy was a writer and journalist, Benoit a photographer. They were travelling through Patagonia, they said, gathering material for a book. Sadly, Benoit's irreplaceable Nikon camera and extra lenses had been stolen from their hotel room in Puerto Deseado on the Atlantic coast, and so all they had to take pictures with was Guy's Pentax. They too were planning to visit the Perito Moreno glacier, but as yet had found no accommodation closer than Calafate. Today's outing to the Upsala glacier was costing them very little, simply because they happened to be staying at the same hotel as the Japanese Peruvians.

To reach the Upsala glacier, we first rode the bus a short distance to a wharf jutting out into Lago Argentino. At the end of the wharf waited a white, many-windowed tour boat called *La Senvera*. As Catherine said later, we should have known the expedition was ill-fated, because just as we were transferring from the bus to *La Senvera*, fog came down and it started to rain. Not only that, a cool breeze sprang up. The Japanese tourists, chattering and pushing, swarmed aboard, taking all the good seats. By the time Catherine and I and the two Frenchmen had negotiated the slippery gangplank, the only seats left were on the lower level, away from the windows.

Not that it mattered.

For one thing, *La Senvera* lacked defrosters. In no time, the windows were completely fogged up. People in advantageous seats used kleenex, handkerchiefs, baseball caps to clear peepholes, through which there was nothing to see anyway, except fog. Guy and Benoit found this enormously amusing. Very French, they said. Catherine and I followed them out on deck, but the wind and rain made it only marginally better than being inside, where, as the atmosphere became fetid, the Japanese Peruvians waxed vociferous. The view was nil no matter where you were, the fog so thick you could barely make out the radar antenna twirling on the wheelhouse roof.

I estimated we were approaching the western end of Lago Argentino and entering the narrow channel known as Brazo Norte, when we began to see small icebergs. As these grew larger and more numerous, *La Senvera* throttled back, until we were barely moving. It was spooky, inching our way blindly along, surrounded by tinkling brash. Catherine said, "Even if we get there, how will we be able to see glaciers? Or anything else?" It's what we'd all been wondering.

Finally we stopped our forward progress altogether. Indoors, cries of protest could be heard. A few passengers stuck their heads out, scowled at the weather, went back in. One of the deck officers, perhaps the first mate, approached and began haranguing us in Spanish. He waved his arms at the fog, shook his finger at the icebergs. When he realized we didn't understand him, he climbed back into the wheelhouse and sent down the cherubic second mate, who might have been his son, and who told us that this was as far as *La Senvera* could safely go. "These fog eez too thick," he said. "Today eez too thick fog. Yesterday is no these thick. Tomorrow is no these thick. Today eez too thick. We go back now."

Judging by the uproar indoors, the same announcement had been made there too.

"But what about the glacier?" Catherine said. "We paid a lot of money to see it. This isn't fair."

The young sailor was unmoved. "Today eez too much fog, too much ice. Yesterday eez no too much. Tomorrow eez no too much. Today eez too much. We go back now."

Sure enough, the ship began to make a slow turn to starboard, and moments later we were pointed in the direction we'd just come. You could still see our track. Dimly through the fog you could also see gulls riding the larger floes, like commuters on a bus.

Catherine caught the sailor by the sleeve as he tried to escape. "How far are we from this famous Upsala glacier?"

"Ocho kilómetros, señora. Eez that way." He pointed vaguely toward the stern.

"And how close did you get yesterday?"

"Ocho kilómetros, señora."

"And the day before?"

"Ocho kilómetros, señora."

"How many times this season have you actually made it to the Upsala glacier?"

"No comprendo, señora."

"How many times this season have passengers actually seen the Upsala glacier?"

"How many tines, señora?"

"How many times?"

"Cero tines, señora. These fog eez too thick. These ice eez too thick. Cero tines."

"Zero times?"

"Cero tines, señora. Tomorrow eez maybe no so thick."

Then he was gone. Indoors there was tumult, as people

Catherine at a sidewalk café on
Avenida San Martin in Calafate.

realized we'd turned back. Passengers came angrily out on deck. In frustration, a few of them snapped pictures of sea gulls riding icebergs.

Back at the Hotel Los Alamos in Calafate, we complained to Domuyo about the glacier scam aboard *La Senvera*. He listened sympathetically, but you could tell he was trying not to laugh. He blamed the weather, the vagaries of nature, the fog, the rain, the icebergs, the narrow channel known as Brazo Norte, the glacier itself, which produced not only the impeding icebergs, but, in his opinion, the dense fog as well. He was not surprised to hear that so far this season no sightseers had actually caught a glimpse of the Upsala glacier. Last year, the closest *La Senvera* had come was three kilometres, on a day when favourable winds had temporarily dispersed both fog and icebergs. Such days were rare. Not to worry, though. If we would like to purchase postcards showing the Glaciar Upsala in all its glory, he had them for sale at two dollars each, or twenty dollars per set. How many in a set? Ten. Stamps not included.

At a noisy restaurant called Todo Suelto we enjoyed trout empanadas washed down with mugs of Quilmes beer, and spent the rest of the afternoon wandering the streets of Calafate. Late in the day we bumped into Guy and Benoit at El Hornito, a sidewalk café on avenida San Martín. We sat in the sun on wicker chairs, sipping chilled Rosales, surrounded not by icebergs, but by Japanese tourists from Peru. What struck us as funny was that they all spoke Spanish.

* * *

Chapter 10.

From Calafate to Hostería Los Notros,
on the shores of Brazo Rico's Iceberg Canal.
Then to Ushuaia, completing the circle.

Our two days at Los Notros, directly across the Canal de los Témpanos from the glaciar Perito Moreno, more than made up for any discomfort or disappointment we'd encountered thus far in Patagonia. If the gods had grounded me after my first glimpse of the glacier, had forbidden further travel, I'd have accepted it and not felt cheated. The usual adjectives—massive, stunning, awesome, breath-taking—did not suffice. Directly in front of us, further away than it looked (as we discovered next day during a cruise on Brazo Rico), the cobalt blue glacier face, five kilometres wide and fifty metres high, set against a backdrop of snowcapped mountains, dominated the skyline. The sight of it stopped you in your tracks, made your mouth fall open. I said it was like being in an IMAX theatre. Catherine said it was like being surrounded by life-size, colour-enhanced photographs.

And it was quiet. As we stepped down from the Interlagos bus that had brought us from Calafate, the very first thing we noticed was the silence. Somehow, with mountain peaks hemming you in like the walls of an amphitheatre and broad rivers of ice filling the valleys, you expected noise. I don't know what kind of noise, but noise. A drum and bugle corps. Angel choirs. Rock bands. Wolf cries. People shouting. Something to accompany the magenta sunset beginning to tint the tallest peaks. It reminded me of Alberta's Lake Louise, seen from the Château, but on a much grander scale. Stupefied, we watched a barn-size slab of ice peel off the glacier and plunge into Brazo Rico. At that distance, the sound it made

Hosteria Los Notros on the shores of Brazo Rico's Iceberg Canal.

was like a rumble of thunder, or a faraway train crossing a trestle. Catherine said she realized now how the surveyor, Francisco Moreno, must have felt in 1877, when he arrived and first laid eyes on the magnificent glacier that would one day bear his name.

When we turned around we found two young people waiting for us on the hotel stairs—a handsome youth in an alpine costume and a girl in dark skirt and apron. They were smiling at us, giving us time to drink in the view. "Buenas tardes," the boy said, reaching for our bags. "Bienvenido. My name is Nico and this is Catalina. Welcome to Los Notros. You like the panorama? Eez ber' beautiful. Eez what people does, firz tine, take the look."

The exterior of the hotel was striking too—pleasingly rustic, yet stately in black and white, walled with windows and showing lots of wood. Its roof bristled with chimneys. But it was the interior of Los Notros you fell in love with. Like your grandmother's parlour, the spacious main lodge possessed a warm, old fashioned look. It had beamed ceilings, dark rafters, polished floors. At one end of the foyer was a warmly lit bar with a stone fireplace. There were lamps in every corner, tapestries, spinning wheels. The reception area and dining room faced the Moreno glacier through floor-to-ceiling windows, in front of which Catherine and I stood and stared like bumpkins at a sideshow.

As soon as we were registered, Nico took us to a separate lodge next door and ushered us into a snug room on the upper level. It had a picture window facing Brazo Rico and the glaciers, which gave the impression of unlimited space. Actually there were two windows, one in the bedroom and one in the bath. This seemed odd, until Nico pointed out that the oversized bathtub was aligned so that two people could sit in it comfortably and look directly out at the glacier. You could do the same thing in bed, of course, and if you looked in the mirror on the bathroom wall, there was the glacier again, only backwards.

Nico knew we were enchanted, knew enough not to turn on the lamps or distract us by talking. Only the highest peaks were catching sunlight now, seemingly floating and tipped with blood. Lower mountains bulked against the sky, then

Nico and Catalina at Los Notros.

magically disappeared in the darkness. The last thing Nico did before leaving was open the side vent on the bedroom window, just to show us how quickly the outside temperature dropped after sunset. The glacial wind, he said, closing the vent and pretending to shiver, blew straight across the Canal de los Témpanos all night, and by morning, even in October, we might awake to find snow on the ground. He said he would see us later at dinner in the main lodge, where a nice table with a view had been reserved for us, and where, at seven o'clock, his duties changed from those of bellhop to dining room waiter.

"Do you know señor Felipe?" Catherine asked him.

"Naturalmente, I know him," Nico said. "Eez my employer. Eez ber' nice man. He hab' the young son, Salado, manager of Los Notros, eez my bess frien'. We go to school many years in Calafate."

"On our flight from Trelew to Río Gallegos," Catherine said, "we were given this card by the pilot. He said he was a friend of señor Felipe."

She handed Nico the business card Captain Colombres had given us. Nico took it, looked at it, shook his head sadly, handed it back to her. "The son of capitán Colombres and the first son of señor Felipe are kill these airplane crash in Paraguay since two years. These very sad tine, you know. These two nice boys. Señor Felipe refuse to fly now. Capitán Colombres, he don't stop to fly because he love it. I never meet these man. But he lose his son with the son of señor Felipe, brother of my frien' Salado. These ber' sad tine, you know."

Our two evenings at Los Notros were the most pleasant I've ever spent anywhere. The days were agreeable too, of course: unhurried meals, invigorating strolls to the lakeshore and about the grounds. Between cocktails and dinner we talked at length with Nico, Catalina and other staff members. Señor Felipe's son, Salado, the manager of Los Notros, invited us into his office, where we thanked him for giving us a nice room on short notice. He said he was happy to receive two

Mountain view from Los Notros.

Canadians, the first he'd ever met, and to oblige his father's friend and air force buddy, capitán Colombres, with whom he himself had flown many times. Since the death of his only son in Paraguay, poor capitán Colombres had been desolate, could not stand to be alone, had developed a constant need to be among people. Salado's father, señor Felipe, was presently in Río Gallegos, checking on his oil investments. He might or might not be back before we departed for Ushuaia. In the meantime, would we like to boat across the Canal of Icebergs to the base of Perito Moreno glacier? Have a closer look? It would be an unforgettable experience, more unforgettable than any glacier we might have seen in Chile or North America. Did we have warm clothes? The boat trip would be cold and windy. He would add our names to the list of passengers for tomorrow. And if we enjoyed ourselves at Los Notros, would we mention this when we got home? Not that the lodge had any summer vacancies from November to March, but he would like to see more North Americans, who, while demanding value for their money, were lavish spenders.

We lingered over coffee at our table by the window, long after the light had faded from the sky and our candle had burned down. Catherine said that even though it was pitch dark out, she could visualize the Perito Moreno glacier, could sense its charismatic presence.

During the night it rained, sleeted and blew a gusty gale. After a hot bath in the oversized tub, we fell asleep listening to frozen precipitation peppering the windows. Expecting to be housebound next day, snowed in, we awoke instead to radiant sunshine. Out our window, across Brazo Rico, surveyor Moreno's mighty glacier looked like a slice of Antarctica sliding down between mountains.

After breakfast we put on our sweaters and jackets and with twelve other people boarded a launch named *Bandera*. After crossing Brazo Rico broadside to the waves, we banged and bumped our way among floating ice cakes into the Canal de los Témpanos. The *Bandera*'s skipper, a dour old man in dungarees, whose English, while comprehensible, was salted

with profanity, informed us that when large icebergs blocked
the channel, boat trips such as his were impossible. Then, he
said, you had to view the glacier from cliffs on the far shore,
where fences had been built to keep people from falling off.
In the old days, spectators used to climb down to the water's
edge for a sea level view, even though this was prohibited.
Why was it prohibited? (He'd anticipated the question.)
Because since 1960, forty people had been drowned by surging tidal waves. Surely not! Oh, yes, indeed. When blocks of
ice the size of battleships fell off the glacier face, they pushed
a tidal wave of water twenty metres high across the channel,
engulfing everyone and everything. The only time the water
rose higher was when these same mammoth blocks of ice
floated down and dammed the narrow channel into Brazo
Rico. If we were interested, he happened to have videotapes
for sale, showing what happened in 1991 when one of these
ice dams broke, releasing six months of pent up water in a
matter of minutes. A raging, kilometre-wide torrent had
flooded everything downstream and drowned sheep and people in its path. Only twenty-five pesos, twenty-five American
dollars, to see on film this amazing calamity of nature.

Fortunately, there were no ice jams that day, nor any tidal
waves. We sailed in close to the glacier, so close that we had
to crane our necks to look up at it. This seemed foolhardy,
given the danger of falling blocks, but the *Bandera's* skipper
evidently judged the risk worth it. He said the odds of being
bombed by falling ice were about the same as being hit by a
meteorite. When he said this in Spanish, the other passengers
raised such a vocal protest that he steered the launch out into
safer waters.

We were not the only vessel afloat on Brazo Rico that
October spring day. As we sailed slowly back toward the landing stage below Los Notros, we looked out and saw our sister
ship, *Onelli*, passing us, and on her stern deck, incredibly,
there stood Guy and Benoit, the two gay Frenchmen. I say
incredibly, because the chances of seeing them on this remote
body of water must have been about the same as being hit by

Catherine at the Perito Moreno glacier.

a meteor. They were still holding hands. They waved back at us, shouted something we couldn't decipher, pointed up at the skyscraper glacier, as though it were the eighth wonder of the world. As we floated apart, they blew us kisses.

The sunset that night was even more spectacular than on the night of our arrival. We sat in front of the fireplace, sipping green dragons, watching the colours change. High on the eastern horizon, frozen rivers oozed imperceptibly down from the Andes, from Chile. From where we sat, it looked as though they were headed straight for us. If we sat there much longer, we'd be crushed. I was surprised, looking around, to see that the room was almost full. Surprised, because no one was talking, and Argentineans are good talkers, especially over drinks around a fireplace. As darkness deepened, the Perito Moreno glacier gleamed coldly white for half an hour, then faded into obscurity. Catherine said she wished there'd been a full moon. For all we knew, there might have been one, hidden behind the encircling mountains. Nico brought us fresh *dragons verdes,* said he hoped we were enjoying our stay and that we'd come back someday. When we told him we were going next to Ushuaia, on Tierra del Fuego, he shook his head. While he would never question a traveler's motives, he could think of no valid reason to forsake the beautiful mountains and green lakes of Parque Nacional los Glaciares. Not for the barren, windswept emptiness of Tierra del Fuego. Which, in all fairness, should belong to Chile, the way the Islas Malvinas should belong to Argentina. No, he would never ridicule a traveler's itinerary. It was not his place to do so. Still, he couldn't help but wonder.

That night it rained and sleeted again. Gale force winds buffeted our windows. Catherine said it felt and sounded like the glacier gods trying to blow us away. If you listened, you could hear their voices, their admonitions. She pictured Zeus hurling thunderbolts from the top of Mount Olympus, bellowing at his brothers, Hades and Poseidon, to come give him a hand. In view of which, the oversized bathtub was the best place to be, and after that, bed.

The same Interlagos bus that had brought us to Los Notros from Calafate took us back again the following afternoon. When we checked into the Hotel Los Alamos, Domuyo, ever personable, said he was surprised to see us, having expected us to fall victim to the Glacier Park's charm and stay there forever.

When we told him we wanted to proceed to Ushuaia, he looked doubtful, as Nico of Los Notros had done. He said he could see no reason to go willingly to Tierra del Fuego, a refuge for convicts and Chileans, where even the native Cape Horn Indians, the Yahgans, had disappeared without a trace. But when he saw that our minds were made up, he shrugged, laughed, washed his hands of us. He was suddenly busy with other things, and as his vacation started that very evening, he referred us to his friend Gregores at the Rotativo Travel Agency on avenido 9 Julio.

Next morning we paid Gregores a visit. He was a thin, bald, bony individual, whose suit hung on him like sacking. He had a terrible bronchial cough, yet smoked cigarettes one after the other. But at least he saw nothing wrong with Ushuaia as a destination. Though he'd never been there, he was sure it must be interesting. It wouldn't be like going to Macchu Picchu or Iguazú Falls, but we could at least see the Beagle Channel, Cape Horn, Isla Navarino. If we took a harbour cruise, we might catch a glimpse of sea lions. And he'd read somewhere that the old penal barracks were now open to tourists three or four days a week.

Fine, we said, but how do we get there?

According to Gregores, there were several options. We could do what I'd done a month earlier—fly south from Río Gallegos. Or we could fly north to Buenos Aires and start from there. In answer to Catherine's question as to whether we could get there by bus, he frowned, lit a cigarette, blew smoke at the ceiling. "By bus, señora? Yes, that is possible, but not easy." First, we'd drive to Puerto Natales in Chile. From there, we'd drive south to Punta Arenas and board the ferry to Porvenir on the opposite shore of Magellan Strait. On a smaller bus and terrible roads, we would drive east to the Atlantic port of Río Grande, then south again on even worse roads to Ushuaia. And how long would all this take? Gregores had no idea. It would depend on how often we stopped en route. Were there hotels in the towns? Certainly, but of questionable quality. Also, the Porvenir ferry crossed the Strait of Magellan only in good weather and at high tide. The roads were mainly mud and gravel, the terrain mountainous. At higher elevations there might still be snow. Would the scenery be worthwhile? He pursed his lips, looked thoughtful, lit a cigarette. That would depend on the fog, would it not? He, personally, would refrain from driving from Río Grande to Ushuaia. That could be a tedious ordeal. Were there no other possibilities? Could one not avoid traveling so far out of one's way through Chile? Well, yes, one could. But as there was no direct highway from Río Gallegos to Ushuaia, one would be obliged to cross the Magellan Strait by ferry at Primera Angostura, catch a bus to the border town of San Sebastián, proceed to Río Grande. Then, as described already, catch a lift to Ushuaia over the Paso Garibaldi. And how long would that take? Again, he had no idea. It would depend on the ferry, on the bus, on the condition of the roads, on mechanical difficulties. Even, to some extent, on police checkpoints. The problem was, Ushuaia was on Tierra del Fuego, and Tierra del Fuego was an island, separated from the mainland by the bothersome Strait of Magellan. Not only that, many highways were not good. The government in Buenos Aires saw little reason to improve them. The tourist season was short. Trekkers didn't drive Jaguars. Though there were some large sheep estancias along the way, some lakes and rivers and wild animals, even some interesting old towns with stormy political pasts (where tourists might or might not be welcome), few foreign sightseers went this way. It wasn't exactly the Silk Road to China. Especially not in June, July and August, when blizzards were frequent. Plus, the only large settlement was Río Grande, which had a population of fifty thousand. So, did we see the problem? Of course we did. The question, was, how best to solve it.

Gregores put flame to a fresh cigarette, coughed till he was blue in the face. "Bueno! But the solution eez simple, señor, señora. I book you on these direct flight Calafate to Ushuaia on these linea aéreas LADE. Eez no expenses, eez still rapido. You arrive maybe three, four hours. No bad roads, no bad bus, no bad policia."

"If it's so expensive," Catherine said through the smoke, misunderstanding him, "why don't we try another airline?"

"Because, señora, there is no other. LADE eez the only one who fly these plane El Calafate to Ushuaia. From Buenos Aires eez difference. From Buenos Aires eez Aerolíneas Argentinas, Kaikén, LAPA, Austral, but from Calafate eez only one, the bess, LADE! Eez less expenses than these bus."

And so we told him to go ahead and book us aboard LADE airlines. When it came to hotels in Ushuaia, he gave us two choices: waterfront or hillside. On the waterfront there was the Albatross. A very nice hotel. I said I'd already stayed there and would prefer something else. Not that I was afraid of encountering Maria Malaspina in person—only her memory.

On Ushuaia's hillside, halfway up the Glaciar Martial road, Gregores knew of two hotels, Las Hayas (the Beeches) and Hotel del Glaciar. He said he would telephone them both. Which he tried to do, but after several fruitless attempts and as many cigarettes, conceded defeat. Instead, he fired up his fax machine. Las Hayas answered immediately: yes, they could give us a nice room with all meals and a view of the Beagle Channel. "We'll take it," Catherine said, just as the Hotel del Glaciar reported No Vacancy.

It was a relief to get out of the smoke and breathe some fresh air. It was also a relief to have our travel plans to Ushuaia finalized. The day had turned warm and sunny, like summer in Muskoka, and we stopped at a restaurant called El Témpano Errante (the Wandering Iceberg?) for beer and pizza. The place was full of noisy young backpackers jabbering away in Spanish, but somehow their exuberance was infectious. Catherine said to me, "So, how does it feel to be heading back to Ushuaia? You've more or less come full circle."

I'd been thinking about that very thing. It seemed strange, yet somehow logical, satisfying. "This time, I'll be seeing it from a different perspective, and sharing my impressions with someone. I'm going to enjoy it much more. Besides, wasn't it Eugene O'Neill who said that a journey's only half a journey till you're back where you started from. It's taken me a month, but here I am."

* * *

Chapter 11.

Back to Ushuaia, Where It All Began

Our noon flight from Calafate to Ushuaia aboard Air LADE (Lineas Aéreas del Estado) was bumpy and at a lower level than my flight a month earlier from Río Gallegos. This time, we flew between layers of puffy, cream-coloured cloud, which, according to Catherine, was like flying over a field of cauliflower. There were occasional bouts of turbulence, during one of which a pale youth across the aisle, traveling alone, threw up in his barf bag. Since the stewardess was busy serving drinks, Catherine went and got the boy a glass of water and a fresh supply of barf bags. He looked sheepish, yet grateful. He said something to Catherine in Spanish and seemed almost on the point of tears. So she sat down in the empty seat beside him and gave him some kleenex and a Gravol capsule. He threw up once more, put his head back and closed his eyes. From where I sat, I could see the perspiration on his brow and upper lip. The flight attendant came by, shook him, asked him if he wanted orange juice or Pepsi. All he did was groan and hold his stomach, and the flight attendant, apparently miffed, went bustling off down the aisle, pushing her drinks cart. When next I looked, the boy's chin was on his chest and he seemed to be asleep. Catherine came back and sat beside me and said what a godsend Gravol was.

Looking out the window on initial approach, descending between rugged peaks before circling out over the Beagle Channel, it seemed to me there was much less snow at higher elevations than there had been in September. Which made sense—we were, after all, a month closer to summer. The sheer-sided valleys looked greener. The hillsides of the Arroyo Grande sported a mustard-yellow tinge. Across the aisle from us, the airsick youth appeared groggy, but otherwise all right. When he saw us looking at him, he managed a drowsy smile, mouthed the word "Gracias" over the roar of the engines. Catherine said to me, "I can't decide whether he reminds me more of my nephew or one of my pupils. If I understood him correctly, he's learning to be a commercial artist and has come down from Calafate to attend his grandmother's funeral."

The landing was a hard one. We hit, bounced, hit again. Looking out the window was like looking at a dust storm. I remembered St-Exupéry's words about the persistent Patagonian winds. After the third or fourth bounce we stuck and slowed down, apparently with still enough airstrip left. As we turned off at a taxiway, all you could see out the window was the storm-tossed Bahia Ushuaia and low clouds scudding by. Just then, in English, the flight attendant welcomed us to Ushuaia, the world's most southerly city. She advised us that the local time was four o'clock, the temperature ten degrees Centigrade, the wind strong enough to blow you off the disembarkation ladder. Thus warned, we zipped up our jackets and followed our fellow passengers out into the gale. As Catherine said later in the terminal building, waiting for our luggage, the surprise wasn't that we'd made a rough landing, but that we'd managed a landing at all.

Surprisingly, there was a minivan from the Las Hayas Hotel awaiting us. Its driver, a bearded, middle-aged gentleman wearing a baseball cap, introduced himself as Honorio and said that the hotel had received a fax from someone named Gregores at the Rotativo Travel Agency in Calafate, advising them to pick us up at Ushuaia airport. "Eez no necessary, señor, señora. We pick up these guest. We hab' taxi ban for these purpose."

Las Hayas, 3 kilometres from town on the paved road up to Glaciar Martial, was the most luxurious Patagonian hotel we'd stayed at. Which was fitting, because it was also to be our last. It was quite new, beautifully furnished, glowing with blond wood. The carpeted foyer, lit by a huge chandelier, was full of orange amancay flowers. We wondered if these were

the same species as we'd seen from the aircraft. The recep-
tionists, two girls in maroon jackets, spoke English with an
Oxford accent and seemed genuinely pleased to see us. They
had name tags on their pockets—Ana and Sara—and said
that we were by no means the first Canadians they'd ever met.
From December till March, they said, the hotel was full of
tourists waiting to board cruise ships bound for Antarctica,
and sometimes there were Canadians among them. In June,
July and August, there were skiers, both downhill and cross-
country. Was the hotel full now? Not quite, but nearly. There
were Germans registered, Japanese, Brazilians, Italians and
Spaniards. Yesterday, they'd even had two Frenchmen, who
had planned to stay a week, but then changed their minds at
the last minute and went on a cruise to Punta Arenas aboard
the *Terra Australis*. Were their names by any chance Guy and
Benoit? Yes, as a matter of fact, they were. Did we know
them? What a coincidence! They had checked out in the
morning, after promising to be back in a week to pay Ushuaia a proper visit. They wanted to see glaciers and the old
prison. Did we know they were gay? Well, we'd suspected.
Were there many such gay people in Canada? Yes, quite a few.
In Argentina, and especially in Patagonia, they were still quite
rare. The same could not be said for neighbouring Chile,
which, from all accounts, was full to overflowing. Would we
like a map of Ushuaia? Did we realize that Ushuaia was on the
same latitude in the southern hemisphere as Ottawa was in
the northern? No, we hadn't realized, but it seemed reasonable. They had both studied geography at school and that's
why they knew these things. They also worked as part time
tour guides in peak season. Speaking of which, would we like
to sign up for a city tour with Honorio? He could also drive
us through the nearby Parque Nacional Tierra del Fuego,
where we would see the remains of a railway built by convicts
eighty years ago. It was, and still is, called the Presidio Railway. Yes, there was plenty to see and do in Ushuaia. We could
visit the ruins of the penal colony in which the famous anarchist writer, Ricardo Rojas, had been imprisoned. Everyone

in the world, even Canadians, must have heard of Ricardo Rojas. (We hadn't.) Or we could spend a day at the fabulous Museo Fin del Mundo on avenida Maipú. Honorio would be pleased to take us, for a modest fee, up to the ski lodge on Glaciar Martial. Or better still, to the legendary Estancia Haberton, an hour's drive east along the Beagle Channel. There we would see a thousand sheep and a village of huts reconstructed in the style of the extinct Yaghan Indians. And if that weren't enough, harbour cruises could be arranged to Isla de los Lobos, where sea lions abounded.

We must have looked overwhelmed, because Ana and Sara suddenly stopped their litany of sidetrips and said that what we should do, what they would do, if they had just flown in from Calafate, was unpack, take a relaxing bath, and enjoy a cocktail in the lounge. Then, at our leisure, it would be time for a candlelight dinner in the sumptuous dining room of Las Hayas, with a splendid view of Ushuaia harbour—the same view as from our room on the second floor. Tomorrow, or the next day, would be soon enough for planning touristic expeditions with Honorio.

Just as at Bariloche, the weather during our stay was superb: sunshine, warm winds, few clouds. Behind every house there sat a skidoo or ATV, yet it was difficult to imagine the streets of Ushuaia plugged with snow. Out in the harbour, grey naval vessels steamed back and forth, apparently on manoeuvres, and the air was full of helicopters. We learned later that a search was being mounted for two missing Australian sailors, whose boat had been found upside down near Isla Almagro.

Over the next three days, we did pretty much everything Ana and Sara had suggested. We spent a morning at the Museo Fin del Mundo, looking at Fuegian artifacts. We took a harbour cruise and sailed up close not only to colonies of basking sea lions, but to the lighthouse I had observed a month ago from the Hotel Albatross. That stormy September night, Maria Malaspina had referred to the flashing beacon as a boundary marker at the edge of the universe. The day I saw

Ushuaia waterfront.

it with Catherine, from the deck of the cruise boat *Piratur*, in bright sunshine, I realized that in reality it was an indestructible stone column, beyond which lay sparkling blue ocean all the way to Antarctica.

We had lunch ashore at the crowded Café de la Esquina, where we finished up with huge bowls of calafate-flavoured ice cream. In the afternoon we walked by the ruins of Grampa MacDonald's prison. In bright sunshine, it looked far less ominous than it had the day I visited it with Maria Malaspina. The dwarfish guard at the gatehouse was gone, replaced by a tall sailor in white hat and dungarees. Thankfully, Catherine said she had no desire to see the jail's interior. In fact, she was against the idea. And so after taking photographs of the crumbling south wall, we went back down to the waterfront and looked in shop windows.

That night we dined lavishly on crab at La Casa de los Mariscos, then telephoned Honorio to come and fetch us home. When he arrived, he said that arrangements had been

Ushuaia Lighthouse, Beagle Channel.

made to take us next day for a drive into the Parque Nacional
Tierra del Fuego. For a small additional fee, Sara, from the
front desk, would sacrifice her day off to act as guide. We
asked if one could not simply visit the park on one's own.
Well, no. Not until the present controversy was resolved.
What controversy was that? Well, the controversy over the
government classification of the park as *reserva estricta.*
Which meant? Which meant that unless you were a bona
fide scientist, you had to be accompanied by a guide. A
licensed guide, who could assure officials that you had no
intention of pitching a tent, stealing bones, or outstaying
your welcome.

Next morning, with Honorio at the wheel and Sara
pointing things out, we paid a large entrance fee to enter the
park. Almost the first thing Sara showed us was the short sec-
tion of narrow-gauge railway, built by convicts between 1909
and 1930. She said that her mother's great-uncle, Héctor
Campora, a presidential hopeful before Juan Péron, had been

incarcerated at Ushuaia prison and had laboured on this useless track that had cost many lives yet led nowhere.

There was silence in the van for a while. As Honorio smoked a cigar, I thought about Grampa MacDonald and the reason I'd come to Ushuaia in the first place.

After passing a checkpoint, at which uniformed guards examined our identification and searched the van, we drove several kilometres along the reedy shore of Lago Roca, on whose surface bobbed small brown geese known as *caunquén*. Coming back, Sara told us that the Parque Nacional Tierra del Fuego had an annoying Canadian connection—beavers. These bucktoothed creatures had been imported and were now a tree-destroying, dam-constructing scourge. She seemed to expect an apology from us, but at the price we were paying for her services, we didn't feel obliged.

Back at the hotel, we cancelled all further trips in Honorio's van. Not that they weren't informative, but the cost was becoming prohibitive.

We spent a relaxed and pleasant afternoon at a window table in the lounge, sipping chilled Gobernador beer, trying to come to grips with the fact that our travels together were all but over. It was not an easy subject to broach. We skirted it by recalling Chiloé, Bariloche, Puerto Montt. We talked about señor Ibañez and little Lucia at Puerto Aguirre. Catherine remembered two Mapuche brothers at Castro, Eben and Cézar, who would not look into the camera but had allowed us to photograph them. Our impressions of Trelew and Puerto Madryn were vivid, but not as vivid as those of the Perito Moreno glacier. We made a contest out of trying to name the hotels we'd stayed at, along with their desk clerks. Somehow, the weeks leading up to Ushuaia seemed telescoped.

After a long silence, Catherine said she'd decided to fly directly home to Ottawa from Buenos Aires. She said she thought it would be best if we parted company before that.

At first, this surprised me. I'd more or less assumed we'd arrange to fly back to Canada together. At least as far as Miami, if not Toronto. But now she was saying she didn't

National Park entrance near Ushuaia.

Brothers Eben and Cézar at Castro.

even want me to accompany her to Buenos Aires. It made no sense. We were going in the same direction, at the same time. Why not enjoy each other's company as long as possible? Was it absolutely necessary that we split up at all?

Evidently it was.

"I have my reasons," Catherine said.

"Which are?"

"I'd rather not say. I doubt I could put them into words properly. Not in a logical way."

We sipped our drinks, stared at the navy ships down in the harbour. Unbidden, the image of Grampa MacDonald sailing from Mar del Plata to Ushuaia in 1915 aboard the *Primero de Mayo* popped into my head. He'd been a sailor all his life, but that was to be his last voyage. I still hadn't mentioned him to Catherine. I decided now that I wouldn't.

"So what you're saying is, you think we should fly back to Buenos Aires on separate airplanes?"

"Yes."

"I can't help but wonder why."

"It would be easier. Anyway, I have to be back in Ottawa next week. You could stay here as long as you like. You don't have to leave just because I do."

Sarcastic comments came to mind, but I said nothing. It occurred to me that since I'd originally arrived in Ushuaia alone, it was only fitting that I leave the same way. I hadn't come here to find anyone, or even socialize. Nothing lost, nothing gained.

"You could go back and see the inside of that prison. Take a trip to the Haberton sheep ranch. Wait for Guy and Benoit."

"But I'd rather fly to Buenos Aires with you."

"Please. I've thought this over. I really have. It's best we do it my way. Trust me."

The waiter, whose name was Guido, brought us fresh beers and a bowl of araucario nuts. Somewhere, someone started playing a piano.

"What I'd like to do," Catherine said, "as soon as I get home, is write you a long letter. That may sound strange, but

I've always been better at writing than talking. Remind me to get your address. I hope you'll answer my letter. All my letters. It would be nice if we could travel together again sometime. Say in the spring. I've been thinking of taking a river cruise from Amsterdam to Budapest, by way of Vienna. I've always wanted to sail on the Rhine and the Danube. That would top my agenda. Or from Piraeus to London and on up to Iceland. The possibilities are endless."

"But not by plane from Ushuaia to Buenos Aires?"

"No. Not right now."

The first clouds we'd seen all day were floating in off the Beagle Channel. Nothing serious, just rolls of cumulus sneaking ashore for the night. Guido went off duty and was replaced by Hipolito. "Señor, señora?" he said, offering to replenish our supply of araucario nuts and bring us fresh beers.

But we turned him down. After a long day, it was time to think about freshening up for dinner.

Next morning under sunny skies we took a taxi to the offices of Aerolíneas Argentinas on avenida San Martín and booked passage to Buenos Aires. The pert young ticket agent, with the name Hilda on her name tag, assuming we were married, thought it strange that we wanted flights on different days. When Catherine asked for connections all the way to Toronto, Hilda mistakenly thought she meant for both of us. She would have printed up two sets of tickets had Catherine not stopped her.

Though the next day's flight was booked solid, there was still space on today's, which left at three o'clock in the afternoon and put passengers into Buenos Aires at nine-thirty. There was a connecting flight to Miami at midnight, which arrived there at ten o'clock the next morning. One could then catch the noon shuttle to Toronto.

It all sounded so rushed, so hectic, that I was sure Catherine would wait a day. But she didn't. She told Hilda to book her straight through to Toronto. She said she was already packed and anxious to get home.

I debated spending another couple of nights at Las Hayas, but ended up checking out when Catherine did. After lunch, we took a taxi to the Hotel Albatross, where I dropped off my luggage, then proceeded to the airport. There wasn't much time for a lengthy farewell. We sat in the crowded, noisy waiting room, not saying much, waiting for Catherine's boarding call. We hugged, kissed, but shed no tears. I gave her my address and phone number, promised to send photographs. When she lined up to go through security, I said I still couldn't believe she was leaving without me. I must have looked lonely, or despondent, or stupefied, because she left the queue and came and gave me a final hug and a longer kiss. People were watching us. Surprisingly, no one took her place in the line-up. They left room for her, let her back in without complaint. Some of them even smiled sympathetically, thinking they understood, when actually they didn't. And then she was gone. There were no windows, and so I got no final glimpse of her. I went into the bar next door, which looked out over Ushuaia's single runway, and sat there until the blue Aerolíneas Argentinas 737 took off. I admit feeling sorry for myself. I was also a little angry. I remember wondering why I'd bothered returning to Ushuaia. I could easily have avoided being left in the lurch by a selfish, impulsive traveling companion, of whom I'd become inordinately fond. Perhaps I should have told her that before she left, should have conveyed my inner feelings. Except that I wasn't entirely sure what they were. In any case, it was too late now. When the bartender asked me what I wanted to drink, I snubbed him, turned rudely away.

I spent that evening and most of the next day walking the waterfront streets of Ushuaia. Search vessels were anchored in the harbour, helicopters came and went. I thought about revisiting the prison, but couldn't quite muster the courage. I did visit a ninety-year-old church on avenida Maipú, the Iglesia de la Merced, on whose doors a bilingual plaque said it had been built using convict labour. I also visited the town library, the Biblioteca Sarmiento, on avenida San Martín. When I came out, I found a craft market in full swing in the parking lot and spent an hour browsing among the stalls. I had pizza for lunch at Café Opíparo, out on the long wharf called Muelle Turístico. On the walls of the café were fuzzy old black and white photographs of Ushuaia harbour in bygone days, showing whaling ships and Antarctic explorers. From my table I could view all the present-day boats in port—tankers, freighters, coast guard vessels—and watched the cruise ship *Marco Polo* come in and begin disgorging passengers.

That evening I ate alone in the dining room of the Hotel Albatross. I don't know if the waiter recognized me or not. He may have. He gave me the same table he'd given me the night I dined there with Maria Malaspina. If he did recognize me, I give him credit for not asking where the young lady was. The young *married* lady from Bariloche, who was waiting for her pilot husband.

As darkness descended, the same lighthouse began flashing at the entrance to Ushuaia harbour. As a matter of fact, the whole harbour was alive with lights. The *Marco Polo* winked and sparkled like a floating casino. Navy ships were smartly outlined. Helicopters whumped overhead. The whole scene looked unreal, unworldly, made me uncomfortable. I wished Catherine were there. When I could stand it no longer, I went to my room, turned on the T.V., ransacked the minibar. Above the bed hung a large, amateurish painting of the very lighthouse that was flashing at me from out of the gloom.

* * *

Chapter 12.

Epilogue: Journey's End

The following day I flew from Ushuaia to Buenos Aires aboard an Aerolíneas Argentinas 737. The flight took just under six hours. We stopped very briefly at Río Gallegos and Trelew.

In Buenos Aires, I checked into the Alvear Palace Hotel and told Reception that if the weather were nice, I'd stay three days.

On the first of those days, I spent the entire morning walking through the Recoleta cemetery. I found the tombs of Eva Péron and Luis Firpo. I also watched a gay pride parade in the park attached to the graveyard, and a children's disorganized, but energetic, soccer game. After the game I talked to a broad-shouldered youth who had a dozen dogs on leashes and made his living taking them for long walks. When I asked him where one could get a good lunch in the Recoleta district, he directed me to a whole string of restaurants across Calle Ortiz, saying they were all superb, but expensive. As I found out for myself, they were.

In the afternoon, I took a city tour by bus, which picked me up and dropped me off at my hotel. I was impressed by the obscenely wide main thoroughfare, avenida 9 de Julio, sixteen lanes across, with its monstrous white obelisk at Plaza de la República. We stopped at a flea and antique market in the suburb of San Telmo, where we were entertained by tango dancers and street musicians. We saw the brightly painted tin houses of La Boca, made a pit stop at a sleazy bar with paper money glued to its walls. The bartender also sold pornographic books and videos. We slowed down to admire the Museo de Arte Moderno, the church of Santo Domingo, the Biblioteca Nacional. Our longest stop was in front of the

Presidential Palace, the austere, dirty-grey Casa Rosado, on Plaza de Mayo. In laboured English, our sharp-voiced guide named the presidents who had inhabited the palace prior to 1966. Why she stopped at 1966, I have no idea. Perhaps recent presidents were an embarrassment. She did say that the palace contained a museum and a basement full of cata-combs, and that we should come back and visit it on our own. The high price of admission was well worth it. Then she pointed at an upper balcony and said that in the movie *Evita*, Madonna had stood there to sing her song. A lady in the seat behind me, who might have been from Texas, asked our guide if the Plaza de Mayo was where the Mothers of the Missing came on Sundays and Thursdays to march in protest and carry placards. Of course we all knew it was, but the tour guide hemmed and hawed and said that every great country had skeletons in its closet, including the United States, which had once allowed slavery, and that someday things would be smoothed over. In the meantime, what we should do, to appreciate the thriving, cosmopolitan city of Buenos Aires, founded by the Spaniards in 1580, was forget about people like Videla and Péron and pay a visit to the Catedral Metro-politana, there, across the Plaza. This was greeted by a mix-ture of chuckles and applause, and the next thing we knew the bus began dropping passengers off at their respective hotels.

Next day I had to choose between a Gaucho Fiesta at a ranch in the countryside, complete with barbecue and demonstra-tion of horsemanship, and a cruise through the myriad chan-nels of the Delta del Tigre. I flipped a mental coin and chose the delta cruise.

First thing in the morning I took a taxi to the Retiro train station, where for the princely sum of $3 I bought a ticket on the commuter train known as Ferrocarril Mitre. The cars on this above-ground subway were shiny and new and only moderately crowded. From my window I had a perfect view of the city as we sped north. I began to appreciate its immense size, its diversity of architecture, its appalling urban slums. In less than an hour we had left all that behind and were into the green and pleasant district known as Tigre. The map in my guide book showed a Medusa-like maze of rivers—Río Luján, Río Paraná, Río Tigre, Río Uruguay—all of which meander finally into the mighty Río de la Plata, on the border between Argentina and Uruguay. I imagined that the Florida Everglades must look like this, or the Okefenokee Swamp, or the bayous of Louisiana.

I disembarked on the outskirts of Tigre, where a hundred beautiful old wooden launches, glistening with varnish and festooned with pennants, awaited passengers. They were tied to rickety piers around a marina, and reminded me of similar craft I'd seen on the Thames in London, England. I wished Catherine had been there to help me choose one. I finally went up to a bristle-haired, elfin-like old man in sunglasses and asked him if he spoke English. He assured me he did. I asked him how much he'd charge for an afternoon of leisurely cruising through the channels of the delta. He said fifteen dollars an hour, minimum two hours. Or, if I preferred, three hours for forty dollars. Better still, four hours for fifty dollars, lunch and commentary included. It was really not possible, he said, to do justice to the Tigre and Paraná deltas in less than four hours. There was too much to see. Too many beautiful riverside houses. Too many beautiful yachts owned by rich people. Too many beautiful women sunbathing. One must cruise methodically and take one's time.

From where I stood, I could see launches with signs advertising prices a bit below his, but for some reason I liked this scurvy old seadog, in his blue cardigan and New Balance sneakers. And so I hired him for the entire afternoon.

He took my money, shook my hand, told me his name was Garcia. He ushered me aboard very formally, opened the boat's windows, pushed back its sun roof. Would I mind, he asked, if other passengers joined us? I said I wouldn't, but in view of the large number of empty boats tied up and waiting, I questioned his optimism. He said that the busy season had

Garcia, boatman on the Delta del Tigre.

not yet started. That today, in fact, was going to be only his third trip of the summer. In another month or so, his and all the other launches would be filled to capacity. Standing room only. Especially in hot weather, when weekenders came from Buenos Aires to cool off. Would I be interested, perhaps, in a crossing to Uruguay? Not in his shiny little motorized gondola, of course, but aboard a fine big ferry to Carmelo or Nueva Palmira. His son was chief engineer. Why, I asked him, would I want to go to Uruguay? He could think of no good reason, and so the topic was dropped. I asked him if he knew a good place along the way for a midday meal, and he said he did—El Gato Blanco, The White Cat. It was on a nicely treed island, not far away, maybe twenty minutes. I asked him where he'd learned to speak English so well, and he said that for most of his working life he'd sailed on American ships. He'd taken night courses one year while stationed in Biloxi, Mississippi. For a sailor, the world was not a large place. He also knew Italian words, French words, German words. He could survive in any port. He'd been to England six times, Australia twice. I asked him if he'd ever been to Tierra del Fuego, and he said no, the furthest south he'd ever been was Mar del Plata. I asked him if he'd tell me about the reign of Juan Péron, and the state of politics nowadays under Carlos Menem. Did I wish him to discuss the massacre of the Montoneros during The Dirty War? The inhuman torture chambers in the Naval Mechanics School of Buenos Aires? Did I wish him to assess Argentina's incredible stupidity and inefficiency during the Falkland's War? Or the nation's shame symbolized by the Madres de la Plaza de Mayo? Should he include a discussion of the ruthless General Jorge Rafael Videla? And of the vast fortunes stolen by certain other generals and deposited in banks in Switzerland? Did I wish him to include the complicity of the Roman Catholic bishops? Is that what I wished him to talk about?

I said yes, that would do for a start. Perhaps as we spent the afternoon cruising among the channels of the delta, he could keep me amused and entertained. That way, he could earn his fifty dollars.

If that's what I'd hoped, I was in for a disappointment. Removing his sunglasses, Garcia said he had no intention of baring his soul, or the soul of Argentina. Especially concerning things that were best forgotten. People from his generation had a right to a little residual paranoia. These days, the walls might not have ears, and dissidents might not disappear into the cellars of the Naval Mechanics School, but even so, he remembered, and his memories were painful.

Having said all that, and knowing very well there were no more passengers coming, he suddenly put his sunglasses back on, threw off the mooring lines, and started his engine. It had a throaty, melodious sound, halfway between a growl and a rumble. We pulled slowly away from the river bank and headed out into midstream. Trees drooped over us. Tall reeds grew along the shore. In no time, there were ducks, herons, kingfishers galore. There were other boats too—rowboats, motorboats, tour boats like ours. We glided over dark brown water, leaving scarcely a ripple. At times, the channel was so narrow and the foliage so thick overhead that it seemed like evening. It was very quiet, very relaxing. The old song, "Flow Gently Sweet Afton" popped unbidden into my head. And then, "Swanee River." And then something about "cruising down the river on a Sunday afternoon." It was, as I say, quite beautiful. I could hardly believe I was in Argentina, an hour north of the noise and pollution of Buenos Aires, where 12 million people swarmed. Yet I felt a certain nostalgia too, a loneliness, almost a sadness. Garcia was fairly good company, a good talker and a fair singer, as I discovered, but the one I missed, let's face it, was Catherine. Had she been there, it would have been perfect. I wondered if Garcia would have charged her fifty dollars too. As we slowed down to pass an oncoming launch full of chattering school children, I asked him. He said yes, of course he would have. That was the price per person for an afternoon. Fifty dollars. Lunch and commentary included. I asked him when the commentary would start, and he said I'd already had most of it. Besides, with only one person aboard, it was hardly worth his while. Surely even I, a tourist from Canada, must realize that. It would be silly for him to pretend to be talking to a multitude.

At the mouth of Río Parana de las Palmas we ducked into a narrow tributary which Garcia said had once been a hideaway for smugglers. Just then a large white tour boat went by, and he said it was on its way to a resort island in the middle of Río de la Plata which until recently had housed deposed presidents and political prisoners. He said that my hotel in Buenos Aires, the Alvear Palace, was named after one such president. He said that the crew of the scuttled German battleship *Graf Spee* had been detained there during the war.

No sooner had he said this than our own boat lost power and slowed to a stop. Garcia grunted, swore, scratched his head. He tapped a few gauges, stuck his head out the window. Finally he opened a hatch in the floor, from which rose a miasma of blue smoke. He reached down with a wrench and made adjustments, then restarted the engine. To me, it sounded rough, uneven, unwilling, like an old man with bronchitis. I could see that Garcia was not happy. He steered us around a corner into a tree-lined creek and there, on the verdant bank, was a low white building with a glassed-in veranda and a large sign facing the river: "El Gato Blanco – Comedor."

"Tine for the lunch," Garcia said, nosing the boat into a mooring between two cabin cruisers.

"Your engine doesn't sound well," I said.

He waved his hands at the clouds of blue smoke rising around him. "Is nothing," he said, laying out an assortment of tools. "While you eat, I fix." When he opened the hatch, you could smell burning rubber. He had to step back to avoid being asphyxiated.

The cool, green patio of El Gato Blanco was a lovely spot in which to enjoy lunch. There were patrons at only three other tables, who didn't even look up as I made myself comfortable and ordered the most expensive item on the menu—mixed grill. I asked the waiter if wine were included, and he said it was, and so I ordered a carafe of vino tinto. The meal was both copious and delicious. So much so that halfway through, after course number three, I ordered a second carafe of wine. As I awaited my tarta de fresa for dessert, I spotted the namesake of the restaurant—a large white cat, sitting imperiously on the flagstones near the door. He was methodically washing his whiskers. Though he was large and spotless, he was much too aloof to remind me of the white cat at the Chilean border post. I called to him, offered him a scrap of barbecued steak, but he ignored me.

After the strawberry tart I had coffee and a dish of pistachio ice cream. I didn't remember ordering it, but the waiter also brought me a snifter of what I believe he called *regaliz*—liquorice liqueur. Fairly glowing with plenitude and contentment, I wandered over to see how Garcia was coming along with repairs to his engine. I found him down under the floorboards, covered in grease, knuckles bleeding, not in a good mood. "Garcia," I said. "Should I call a taxi?"

On the patio at El Gato Blanco, Delta del Tigre.

I thought it was funny, the idea of ordering a taxi on an island in the middle of a delta, but Garcia evidently did not. He grumbled, swore, banged his wrenches together. I believe he mentioned the cursed fan belt. Or it might have been the flywheel. Or the water pump. In any case, repairs were far from complete. If I would be patient and go and sit down somewhere, he would come and find me.

So I did. I went back to my shady table on the patio and ordered a second regaliz. With ice. It cost extra, but what the hell. I wasn't paying for it.

As it turned out, I was.

At the end of the second hour, the waiter, Chaiquil, who I gathered was also the proprietor, presented me with an astronomical bill. One hundred and ten pesos. I said, "I'm on señor Garcia's boat. I've paid for the afternoon, which includes commentary and lunch. He'll take care of this."

Which made Chaiquil laugh uproariously. "No, señor," he said. "You have misunderstand. Lunce included with Garcia mean tine for lunce, but not prize for lunce. These you muz pay youself. Eez no include in prize. Lo siento. I sorry for you, but you muz pay these."

So I went back to the boat and asked Garcia if this was true, and he said it was. Why, he asked, would he pay for my lunch? If he had a boatload of passengers, was he expected to buy lunch for all of them? Don't be ridiculous. As to the repairs, another hour might see them finished. Which would give us just enough time to get me back to the marina from which we'd started three hours ago, so that I could catch my train to Buenos Aires.

I said I didn't think that was fair. I'd had no delta tour to speak of, just three hours on an island waiting for him to fix his engine. Not only that, I'd had to buy my own lunch, after being told that lunch was included. It seemed to me, I said, that I was entitled to a partial refund.

Garcia clanked his wrenches, threw rotted sections of rubber hose out of the engine compartment. He had globs of grease on his face, in his hair. His blue sweater was a mess, as were his trousers. But the most notable thing, in my humble opinion, was that magically, instantaneously, he'd lost his ability to speak English.

I'm not complaining, really. I enjoyed the afternoon. Before the engine breakdown, I'd been thinking that another three hours of meandering about the lagoons and tributaries of sluggish rivers was going to get boring. True, there were things to look at—big trees, sprawling houses, beautiful yachts, but a surfeit of these things could lull you to sleep. Had I been given a choice, I'd have opted for a long, leisurely lunch at El Gato Blanco, sitting on the patio, watching other boats go by, wondering if they were owned by smugglers, or by insurgents bent on overthrowing the government, or by corrupt ex-presidents on their way into exile. As I counted out my money for Chaiquil (he preferred cash to credit cards), I handed him my camera and asked to snap my picture to prove I'd been there. Which he obligingly did, as he would have done for any tourist. Was that his white cat? Yes, it was. Actually, he had four white cats. All brothers and sisters. Their names were Tigre, Perdriel, Estela and Isabelita. They kept the place free of los ratóns. I didn't know if los ratóns were mice or rats.

The afternoon was wearing on, the sun dropping behind the tallest trees before Garcia finally got his engine started. I was walking along the riverbank when I heard it rumble into life. When I was back aboard, I asked him why he hadn't phoned or radioed for a replacement boat to come and pick me up. For one thing, he hadn't thought of it. He'd been too busy. For another, he had no phone, no radio.

I was amazed at what a short distance we'd actually covered. After leaving El Gato Blanco, we made two or three turns, nipped through a side channel, and there was the marina from which we started out several hours previously. Looking at his watch, Garcia said that if I hurried, I could catch the next train back to the city. I thanked him for his commentary and his singing and said I hoped his boat stayed healthy. I would have shaken his hand, until he showed me how dirty it was. "Come back tomorrow," he said. "I'll take you for a nice cruise through the Delta del Parana. Fifty dollars for the afternoon, lunch included."

I shook his hand anyway, because he reminded me of my father. "Tomorrow," I said, "I fly back to Canada. My holidays are over. I've been away a long time. But if I ever come back to Buenos Aires, I'll take you up on that."

* * *

As I write this, I'm halfway to Miami on an Aerolíneas Argentinas 747. The captain has just announced that we've left Bolivian airspace and are now over Río Branco, Brazil. I'll take his word for it. It seemed like a crooked trajectory to me, until I remembered that while we're in the air, the earth keeps spinning. Down below, all I see is rain forest. We could be anywhere. Thank God for GPS. I spent the first three hours of the flight napping and composing a note to Catherine, telling her what I'd been doing since leaving Ushuaia. It turned out to be a lengthier list than anticipated. I told her I wished we could have seen Buenos Aires together. I also told her I'd very much like to accompany her on a cruise from Amsterdam to Budapest in the spring. Or anywhere else, for that matter.

I hope that when I get home there's a long letter from her. I'm sure there will be. It's what she promised. If there isn't, I just might disobey instructions and hop a plane to Ottawa.

* * *

AGMV Marquis

MEMBER OF SCABRINI MEDIA

Quebec, Canada
2001